MIND TOOLS

Also by Fred Bortz

Superstuff! Materials That Have
Changed Our Lives

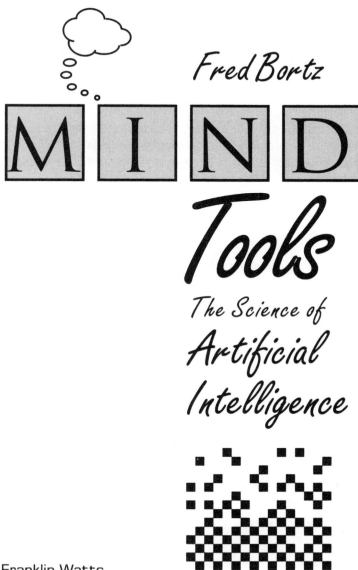

Fred Bortz

MIND
Tools
The Science of
Artificial
Intelligence

Franklin Watts
New York / Chicago / London / Toronto / Sydney
A Venture Book

DEDICATION

To Susan, who uses her knowledge base and natural intelligence in an unending quest for wisdom

Grateful acknowledgment for permission to reprint these figures goes to: MIT Press: p. 15; Jeff Pepper: p. 61; The Association for Computing Machinery: p. 47.

Photographs copyright ©: The Computer Museum, Boston, MA: pp. 1, 6; International Business Machines: p. 2; Charles Babbage Institute/Crown: p. 3; Carnegie-Mellon University: pp. 4, 5 top, 7; Massachusetts Institute of Technology/Donna Coveney: p. 5 bottom; University of Rochester/James Montanus: p. 8; Lou Jones: pp. 9, 14; Rainbow Inc.: pp. 10 (Dan McCoy), 11, 15 (both Hank Morgan); The Robotics Institute, Carnegie-Mellon University: pp. 12, 13; Intel Corporation: p. 16.

Library of Congress Cataloging-in-Publication Data

Bortz, Fred
    Mind tools: the science of artificial intelligence / by Fred Bortz.
        p.   cm.—(A venture book)
    Includes bibliographical references and index.
    Summary: Discusses the science of artificial intelligence including the development of the computer and its importance in day-to-day life.
    ISBN 0-531-12515-7
    1. Artificial intelligence—Juvenile literature.   2. Computers—Juvenile literature.   [1. Artificial intelligence. 2. Computers.]
    I. Title.
Q335.4.B67   1992
006.3—dc20   92-16653 CIP AC

Contents

MIND TOOLS

Prologue: Beyond the Outer Limits of Our Minds

We humans are not the fastest living beings on our planet, nor are we the strongest. Our vision is not the best, nor is our hearing or our sense of smell. We can't swim or jump as well as many other creatures, and we can't fly at all. Yet, despite our physical limitations, we rule this planet. How can that be?

The answer begins with our superior brains, but it doesn't end there. To survive and spread throughout the world, members of our species had to learn how to protect themselves from harsh environments and from dangerous, physically superior beasts.

Our brains gave us language, but a person's words could not persuade a wolf not to attack. Nor could a hunter talk a bear out of its warm fur.

Superior brains enabled humans to think of farming. But thoughts do not move earth, plant seeds, or control the flow of water.

Imagination led people to try to understand the sun, moon, stars, and planets; to want to fly higher than the birds; to dream of swimming to the ocean floor and running faster than gazelles.

But language, thoughts, and imagination alone

can't take us beyond our physical limits. Tools can. Tools enable us to change our environment and to take advantage of the forces of nature.

TOOLS AND THE HISTORY OF CIVILIZATION

According to many historians, tools have been a major cause of the great changes in human history. Civilization began with the simple tools of prehistoric people more than 2 million years ago and developed as tools became more advanced. About 8000 years ago, agricultural civilizations emerged, and soon those early farmers devised tools that took advantage of their own abilities and the greater strength of animals.

In recent centuries, civilization took a dramatic turn as steam-powered tools and machines launched the Industrial Revolution. Today's world of gasoline engines and electrical devices is changing faster than any previous society changed. Because of today's tools, we have gone far beyond the physical limitations of living bodies.

So you might be tempted to say that we can now go as far as our minds can take us. That's wrong—we can go further! For besides developing tools that assist our bodies, humans have been developing tools that assist our minds.

MIND TOOLS AND THE FUTURE

The development of mind tools actually began long ago when the first human drew a picture to share information with someone else. From that day onward, human ideas could be preserved in something other than brains. After pictures came written language and then the development of books and printing, which made it possible to preserve information and spread it throughout the world.

Books and other written materials are mind tools that enable us to go far beyond the limitations of human memory. Mind tools of a different kind—computers—have more recently enabled us to do the same with calculation and computation.

More than that, computers have led us to a revolutionary new way of looking at information and the way it is processed. In fact, most historians believe that this information revolution will be as significant for civilization as was the Industrial Revolution.

Today, as computer systems can hold and process more and more information faster and faster, people are developing new classes of mind tools through a new science called *artificial intelligence* (AI). These new mind tools promise to enhance the capabilities of our minds as much as the tools and mechanical devices of the Industrial Revolution extended our physical capabilities.

This book is written as a guide for a fantastic journey. It explores regions of artificial intelligence that are beyond the outer limits of our human minds. Pay careful attention along the way, for when you have traveled as far as this book can take you, it will be your turn to lead your own expedition into an exciting and unpredictable future.

1
Can Computers Think?

It isn't hard to make a computer look smart. But it isn't hard to make it look stupid, either. Think about a computer program to play the simple game of ticktacktoe. If you have played that game for a while, you have probably figured out how to avoid losing and how to win every time your opponent gives you a chance.

Your winning ticktacktoe strategy is fairly easy to describe in the form of a computer program. So if you know a computer programming language, such as BASIC, you can imagine writing a program that makes the computer play ticktacktoe as well as you do. Of course, if you wanted to be contrary, you could just as easily write a program that makes mistake after mistake, almost forcing the computer to lose.

Although another person might call the computer smart when it ran the winning program and stupid when it ran the losing one, you would know that it is the same machine in both cases. But you would have to agree that the computer behaves, at least when it plays ticktacktoe, like an expert or a bumbler, depending on which program is running.

CREATING A TICKTACKTOE EXPERT

Let's look in more detail at how you would go about creating a ticktacktoe expert computer. First, if you were not a ticktacktoe expert, you would have to become one or find someone who was. Then you would put that expert's knowledge in a form suitable for a computer to use (Figure 1).

Next you would test your creation by putting it into the computer and starting the ticktacktoe game. If the computer made a mistake (either losing to its opponent or failing to make a play that would lead to victory), you would look into what caused the mistake, then correct the problem. You would repeat this sequence of testing and correction until all the errors or "bugs" were removed.

In the end, the computer, using your "debugged" representation of expert knowledge, would always play ticktacktoe intelligently. You could then say that you had "captured" an expert's knowledge and placed it in the computer. You would have created "artificial intelligence."

AI = ARTIFICIAL INTELLIGENCE

Artificial intelligence has become such an important field in computer science that it is frequently referred to simply by its initials, AI. It is also a controversial field, because when we talk about an intelligent computer, we wonder whether we are describing a machine that thinks for itself.

If you have ever written a computer program, you know that computers do their work by following, step by step, a set of simple instructions. That's a long way from thinking. Or is it? What if those sim-

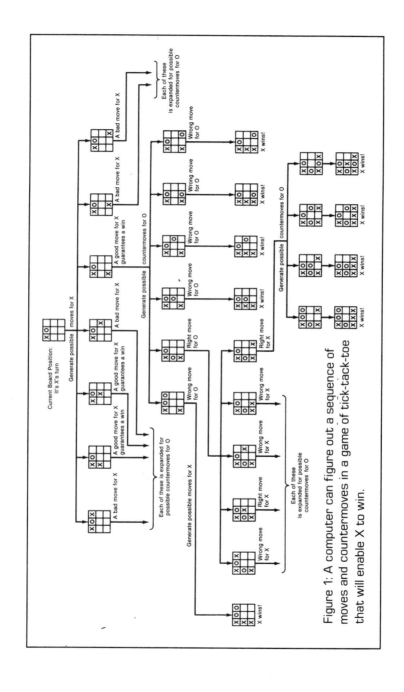

Figure 1: A computer can figure out a sequence of moves and countermoves in a game of tick-tack-toe that will enable X to win.

ple instructions are instructions about how to think? Is the computer intelligent then?

The key question is this: Is it possible now, or might it be possible in the future, to build a computer and write instructions that would turn it into a thinking machine? You may have picked up this book because you were hoping to find the answer. So here it is: Some AI experts say yes, some say no, some say maybe!

Now when experts disagree on the answer to your question, you may feel confused but you know that your question is a very good one. This one is especially good because not only do the experts disagree about the answer, they also disagree about what is being asked. The best answer to the question, Will computers ever be able to think?, may be, It depends on what you mean by thinking.

The next chapter describes the Turing test, which many people consider the best attempt to answer that unanswerable question. But most of this book has another purpose: to tell you something about computers, a little about human brains, and quite a bit about artificial intelligence and the people who work in that field.

You will learn what has been accomplished in AI and what can be accomplished in the future. You will read about "expert systems" that help people in their jobs, about chess-playing machines that can beat all but the very best humans, about computers that can see, about robots that will rove on other planets, and about computers that understand speech and translate languages. You will also read about new technologies that may revolutionize AI and share the vision of AI's future as seen by two of its leading experts.

When you are finished, you'll understand why

most people who work with AI care more about building good mind tools than about whether their computers can pass the Turing test.

So can computers think? Most AI people say, Who cares? What do you think of that!

2

The Turing Test of Machine Intelligence

DEFINING AI

This book uses the most common definition of *artificial intelligence:* behavior performed by a machine that would be considered to require some degree of intelligence if done by a human. This definition separates "intelligence" from capabilities that can be achieved by blindly carrying out a procedure.

By this definition, even "number crunching" that would take hours to perform on a supercomputer is not AI. Likewise, the definition rules out feats of memory such as being able to repeat a chapter of a textbook word-for-word without error.

THE REQUIREMENT OF UNDERSTANDING

Our definition of AI requires that the machine be able not only to store and manipulate information but also to deal with its "meaning." AI requires what we might call interpretation or understanding. To illustrate that point, let's think about how three very different people might go about solving the following problem in a statistics textbook:

If, on the average, a hen and a half lays an egg and a half in a day and a half, how many eggs would you expect six hens to lay in a week?

First, think about giving the problem to Brian, who is a whiz at calculation. You can give him the most complicated computations and, like a computer, he will carry them out quickly and flawlessly every time. But if Brian is no more than a "human calculator," he may be totally unable to turn this question into the simple formula that produces the right answer,[1] no matter how long he looks at it. (That formula is given later in this chapter. You might enjoy thinking about this problem and seeing whether you can come up with the formula yourself before you read that far.)

Even if you would show him that calculation, Brian might not understand how to connect it to the problem. If that were so, you would not judge him to be intelligent, despite his remarkable computation skills.

Now suppose you gave the problem to Rosie, who has an incredible memory. Once she has read a book, she can recite any paragraph on any page perfectly on demand. Rosie might use her remarkable memory to memorize the book, including all the pages in the back where the answers to the problems are printed. Then, if someone were to tell her where and on what page the answer could be found, she would quickly call it out from memory. She could do that without understanding the meaning of what she was saying or knowing anything about numbers or mathematics.

Would you judge Rosie to be intelligent because she knew the answer to this problem? Not if you knew how she found it!

Finally, suppose you gave the problem to Karen,

a student whose ability in mathematics is slightly better than average. She would probably spend a few minutes puzzling over it. After a while, she would come up with a formula that she thought would give the right answer. She would then carry out the calculation in her formula to produce an answer.

If the formula were correct, and if she carried out the calculation correctly, Karen would get the right answer. But even if her formula were wrong or she made a mistake in arithmetic, you would judge Karen to be intelligent because she was grappling with the meaning of what she read.

THE TURING TEST: HUMAN OR COMPUTER?

Now suppose that Brian, Rosie, and Karen are in a different room than you, and you are allowed to communicate with them only through a computer terminal. Furthermore, suppose you are not told whether they are humans or computers, but you are allowed to ask them whatever questions you wish. Finally, suppose that you are challenged to figure out who is who or what.

You start with the hen and a half problem, and you get these answers:

BRIAN: *I don't know.*
ROSIE: *Twenty-six.*
KAREN: *Twenty-eight.*

Although one question isn't enough to determine for certain who is human, your thinking might go something like this: Computers always give the right answer, and since Rosie's and Karen's answers are different, at least one of them is incorrect. Thus at most one of them is a computer, and the one who gave the wrong answer is human. Brian is probably human, although he may be a computer programmed to respond, "I don't know," whenever he cannot interpret the question.

Now you ask a second question: "Please explain your answer." This time they reply:

BRIAN: *I don't know.*

ROSIE: *The answer to problem 7 on page 125 is found on page 478, line 34. Page 478, line 34, contains "26."*

KAREN: *To find the number of eggs produced, take the number of eggs per hen per day, multiply that by the number of hens to get the number of eggs per day, then multiply that by the number of days. In this case, since per means "divided by," we calculate in this way: One and a half eggs divided by one and a half hens divided by one and a half days is two-thirds of an egg per hen per day. Multiply that by six hens to get four eggs per day. Multiplying that by seven days gives the answer: 28 eggs.*

This time, Brian's answer doesn't fit the question very well; so you are beginning to think not only that he is a computer but that his program is not a very clever one.

Karen's answer is very carefully and precisely explained, and it is correct. If she is a computer, her program is a very good one. You'll need to ask some more questions before you can decide.

Rosie's original answer of 26 is incorrect, so you might be inclined to think she is human. But the language used in her explanation seems more like a computer's than a human's. The answer in the back of the book may be wrong; if so, Rosie is probably a computer.

You could go on asking questions, and it wouldn't take you very long to decide that Karen is human and Rosie and Brian are computers—or at least have brains that act as computers do. This game can be very entertaining, but, like many games, it also presents another side to computer scientists.

Since the earliest days of computing machines, people have wondered, Can this machine think? The best way to answer that question, most computer scientists now agree, is to put the computer to a test of "Guess who's thinking, human or computer?"

That test is called the *Turing test* after the British mathematician Alan Turing, who first suggested its use in a famous 1950 article. Turing recognized that it is impossible for people to agree on an exact definition of "thinking," although they know what it is when they see it.

A LIMITED TURING TEST

Turing knew that it would be a long time before any computer could pass his test, but he argued that the test was still useful in many ways; for example, soon machines that could pass the test in a limited area of knowledge or skill would be built.

Today, for instance, people are working to make it possible for a computer to translate English legal documents into Japanese. Because legal language is limited and precise, that task is a lot easier than translating everyday English. Still, a person who translates from one language to another has to think. When the day comes that a Japanese lawyer cannot distinguish between computer-translated and human-translated documents, the computer will have passed a limited Turing test. A more difficult limited Turing test would require the computer to fool a Japanese lawyer who was also a computer expert.

The Turing test makes us think about the many different elements of intelligence and other actions that the human brain can perform. Passing the Turing test requires a particular form of artificial intelligence that we can call artificial thinking, in which computers can mimic certain abilities of the human mind. But for many people, the most exciting part of AI is learning to use the superhuman abilities of computers, such as Brian's amazing mathematical skills and Rosie's super memory, to make mind tools: machines that enhance our brains just as scissors, shovels, motors, and other devices enhance our motor skills.

3

Hardware, Software, and Wetware

To understand how mind tools work, you must first understand the similarities and differences, the strengths and weaknesses, and the structure and operation of brains and computers. Let's start with some basic facts.

HARDWARE + SOFTWARE = PIPSY

Computers are machines made of interconnected electrical, mechanical, and electronic parts or *components*. The components work together as a *system* to do a job. That job is to take *information* in one form, usually called *input*, and to manipulate or *process* it to produce new information called *output*. The processing usually involves combining or modifying pieces of information according to a recipe or procedure called a *program*. The program can work with information that comes in as input, information that is stored in a part of the computer called *memory*, or information that is contained in the program itself.

A simple aid to understanding this is the word *PIPSY*, which stands for *programmable information-processing system*. Let's take that word apart to see what distinguishes a computer from other machines (Figure 2).

Starting from the *SY* at the end of PIPSY, the mechanical, electrical, and electronic parts that make up the computer system are usually called *hardware* because they are solid and substantial, like items you might buy at a hardware store. The word *hardware* doesn't distinguish computers from other machines: from drills and eggbeaters to cars and lawn mowers, all machines are made of hardware.

Backing up to the *IP*, not every machine is an information processor, but a large number are. In their own way, ordinary typewriters, printing presses, and adding machines process information.

It is the first *P* in PIPSY that distinguishes computers from all other machines; computers are programmable. The programs that they carry out, unlike their hardware, are varied and easily changed, making computers very versatile. Because of the ease with which programs can be changed, they are often called *software*. Other machines are made of hardware alone. But the hardware of computers cannot function without software. With software, the hardware of computer systems can be many things, including mind tools.

WETWARE

In many ways, your brain behaves as a computer does. It receives input information from the outside world in the form of electrical signals that travel along your nerves from all parts of your body. Then it produces output information in the form of other electrical signals that enable you to respond to the input (Figure 3).

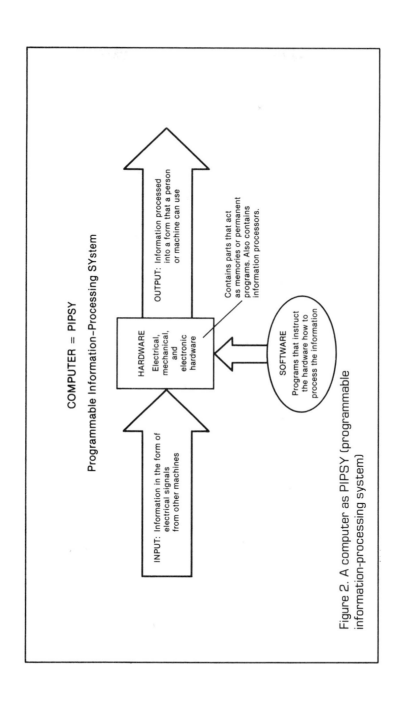

COMPUTER = PIPSY

Programmable Information-Processing SYstem

INPUT: Information in the form of electrical signals from other machines

HARDWARE

Electrical, mechanical, and electronic hardware

OUTPUT: Information processed into a form that a person or machine can use

Contains parts that act as memories or permanent programs. Also contains information processors.

SOFTWARE

Programs that instruct the hardware how to process the information

Figure 2. A computer as PIPSY (programmable information-processing system)

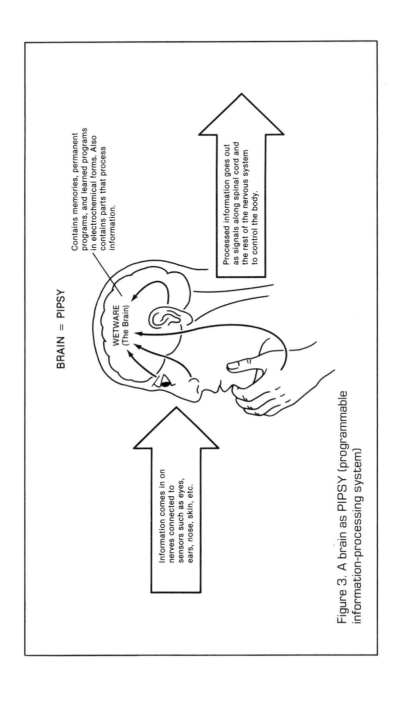

BRAIN = PIPSY

Contains memories, permanent programs, and learned programs in electrochemical forms. Also contains parts that process information.

WETWARE
(The Brain)

Processed information goes out as signals along spinal cord and the rest of the nervous system to control the body.

Information comes in on nerves connected to sensors such as eyes, ears, nose, skin, etc.

Figure 3. A brain as PIPSY (programmable information-processing system)

Suppose, for example, that you are confronted by a snarling dog. Signals from the retinas of your eyes travel along the optic nerves to a part of the brain that interprets them as a visual image. Other signals travel from your ears to the part of your brain that processes them as sounds. Because you have seen and heard snarling dogs before, other parts of your brain, including those that serve as your memory, enable you to recognize the patterns of light and sound as a dog that is threatening to harm you. The result of all this processing is a set of output electrical signals along nerves to muscles and other organs that cause your body to respond to the threat in an appropriate way. Your response is part instinctual and part conscious.

Notice that your brain, like a computer, processes information by combining input signals with internally stored information according to a program. Unlike a computer, the brain is not made of hardware; rather, it is composed of a complex biological substance, shaped in a complicated way, and bathed in a constantly changing electrochemical soup. We could call it *wetware.*

The instinctual part of your response, being inborn, is probably connected with your brain's structure and chemistry. It is like the built-in software that computers need to start up or to carry out routine operations. The conscious part of your response results from a "program" created by your experiences and your ability to learn.

Your brain, like a computer, can be thought of as a PIPSY. In many ways, such as its ability to interpret images and form concepts, it is highly advanced in comparison to a computer; but in a few ways—particularly its tendency to forget or misremember and its limited computational speed and ability—it is primitive. Some AI researchers try to build mind tools that enable people to benefit from the computer's superhuman capabilities. Others seek new ways to build hardware and write software based on research into how human wetware processes its information. You will encounter both types of researchers in this book.

THE FIRST CALCULATING MACHINES

For most of human history, our hardware consisted of tools, machines, and devices that enhanced our physical abilities or eliminated the need for a person to do physical work. But in 1617, John Napier invented the first machine designed to eliminate mental work. Napier's device included a set of movable rods on which digits were printed in a particular pattern. A person could, by manipulating the rods, perform addition, subtraction, multiplication, or division. The rods were often carved from bone; hence the invention was called "Napier's bones."

Napier's bones differ from an abacus in a significant way. When a person uses an abacus, the machine merely keeps track of results while the person's manipulations carry out the arithmetic. When a person uses Napier's bones, the mechanism itself carries out the arithmetic.

Other calculating machines followed Napier's, each one designed to eliminate the tedious, error-prone work of humans performing arithmetic calculations. The most remarkable of these, called the "difference engine," was designed in 1821 by Charles Babbage. The difference engine, everyone agreed, would revolutionize the computation of mathematical tables. Since accurate tables were becoming increasingly important in astronomy and navigation, the British government paid Babbage to turn his idea into an actual machine.

Unfortunately, Babbage's work went astray for two reasons: the machine and its inventor! The design of the difference engine was so complex that it was nearly impossible to build. With each complication Babbage encountered, the project grew more difficult to manage and the machine became more costly. At the same time, Babbage let himself become distracted by his latest inspiration. Instead of concentrating on building the difference engine, he began to design a much more powerful machine, which he called the "analytical engine."

The analytical engine could not only perform calculations but be programmed to carry out a series of calculations in any order. It was a PIPSY! Unfortunately, building it required parts made with greater precision than was possible at the time. Besides that, it was more complex than the difference engine.

So was Babbage's analytical engine a bad idea? Not at all! In fact it was a great idea, nearly a century ahead of its time. To this day, the operations of most computers are based on the principles of Babbage's dream machine, redesigned to use electronic parts instead of mechanical ones!

THE INVENTION OF SOFTWARE

Babbage's difficulties with the difference engine were complicated by personal tragedy; his father, his wife, and two of his children died during the time he was working on it. Instead of concentrating on the job at hand, he responded to his hardships by becoming obsessed with the grand possibilities of the analytical engine.

Joining him in this obsession was a beautiful young woman, Ada Augusta, countess of Lovelace, who was, incidentally, the daughter of the renowned British poet Lord Byron. While Babbage concentrated on the machine itself, Lady Lovelace developed fundamental ideas for writing and applying the programs. In today's computer terminology, Babbage worked on the hardware while Lovelace concentrated on the software.

Lovelace's notes from that time include her speculations, as well as Babbage's, that machines based on the analytical engine might someday play chess, compose music, and carry out other tasks that would normally require a great deal of human thinking. She was probably the first person to ask the question, Can computers think? Her answer was no because she regarded thinking as a mental rather than a mechanical process. Still, she foresaw the day when artificial intelligence would transform the computer into a tool to extend the human mind, regardless of whether the machine were truly thinking.

The story doesn't end there. Tragedy struck again when Lovelace's painful death of cancer at age thirty-six left Babbage alone once more. He died in 1871 with neither of his grand machines completed after a half-century of work, feeling that he had never had a happy day in his life. Only a few mourners attended his funeral.

Today we look at Babbage's obsession with his ambitious designs not as a tragedy but as a triumph. He is credited with laying the foundations for today's computer hardware, and Lovelace is recognized for her pioneering ideas that opened the road to software and artificial intelligence.

THE BRAIN AS A THINKING MACHINE

Babbage and Lovelace speculated about thinking machines, but they did not view the brain as one. If they lived today, they might draw a different conclusion.

We now know that the human brain is made up of about 100 billion interconnected units called *neurons* which communicate with one another by sending electrical pulses. The brain is filled with and bathed in a complex chemical soup, which is constantly changing under the influence of hormones, proteins, and other substances. The behavior of each neuron depends on its chemical and electrical environment.

Although the brain's behavior as a whole is very complex, an individual neuron's behavior is much simpler. A neuron receives a series of electrical signals from other neurons; in computer terminology, these can be considered "inputs." It responds to those inputs according to principles of chemistry and physics. The net result of that response is that the neuron sends electrical signals to another set of neurons; in computer terminology, those are "outputs." From this point of view, a neuron is a simple electrochemical circuit element, and the brain is a thinking machine made up of a huge number of these elements interconnected.

People who take that view often state that the human brain evolved under circumstances where certain substances were present and certain interconnections were able to develop. They argue that different circumstances could have led to the evolution of a very different but "functionally equivalent" brain. If you could replace an organism's present brain with a functionally equivalent one, the organism's behavior would not change. For a human being, that would mean that all memories and thought processes, as well as all physical behavior, would be retained after brain replacement.

Hans Moravec, in his book *Mind Children*, describes a future world in which computer technology is so advanced that it is possible to replace a person's brain with a functionally equivalent computer. Most scientists do not go so far as Moravec. Some, in fact, take the opposite point of view. In his book *The Emperor's New Mind*, Roger Penrose uses principles of physics to argue that it would be impossible to build a machine that was functionally equivalent to a brain. (For more information on these two books, see "For Further Reading.")

4

Two AI Pioneers Look Back on Their Science

When a person discovers a new science, does he or she realize the importance of the achievement? The AI pioneer and Nobel Prize-winning scientist Herbert Simon did.

In his autobiography, *Models of My Life*, Simon describes the excitement he felt as he broadcast the news of the Logic Theorist (LT) program, which found proofs of famous statements in mathematical logic. Simon writes that one of his students at Carnegie Institute of Technology (now Carnegie-Mellon University) recalls that he walked into class one day in January 1956 and announced, "Over the Christmas holiday, Al Newell and I invented a thinking machine."

Some people might have considered the announcement a bit premature since the LT program wasn't even running on the computer at that time. But Simon and his students Allen Newell and Clifford Shaw knew precisely how to write it.

More than thirty-five years later, Simon and Newell are still together at Carnegie-Mellon and still among the leaders of the field that they helped to create. In an interview with the author, Simon and Newell reflected on the early days of AI and looked ahead to its future. This chapter describes the history of AI as seen through their eyes. Their ideas about the future of their science appear in the closing chapter.

AI, LT, AND GPS

In the early days of AI, Simon and Newell weren't thinking about inventing mind tools; they were simply scientists who wanted a better understanding of the way the human mind deals with ideas and concepts. Realizing that they couldn't get inside the human mind to conduct detailed experiments, they sought to do the next best thing: create a model that behaves like the mind, a model that they could study in detail. Their model, they decided, could be a computer program.

Making such a model required a revolutionary change in the way people viewed computers. Simon and Newell recognized that the heart of computation is the process of manipulating symbols. Furthermore, they viewed human thinking as the process of manipulating concepts. Since concepts can be represented by symbols (addition by the plus sign, for example), they said, then computers could be programmed not only to calculate but also to think in humanlike ways. That idea was the beginning of Simon and Newell's search for artificial intelligence.

"We were interested in getting a program that would exhibit intelligent behavior in the sense that it would do something that people have to use intelligence to do," Simon explains. "We scrounged around a little bit in the fall of 'Fifty-five for the right task to try."

Newell adds, "The three tasks that came up were proving theorems [mathematical statements of truth] in logic, proving basic theorems in geometry—that is doing classical high school level geometry—and playing chess. All of these are characterized as being reasoning tasks. And there was the notion of the computer's representing all these situations, not just crunching numbers. Computation isn't foreign to intelligence, but it's not of the essence.

"Another characteristic of our example was that there shouldn't be a well-known systematic way of always getting the answer," Simon continues. "It wouldn't have been fun to write a program that would solve algebra equations because there's a well-known way." In other words, discovery is not necessary for performing algebraic calculations and without discovery, few people would say that the program was intelligent.

"We didn't settle on the logic task until November," Simon says. "This was the task to get a system to *discover* a proof for a theorem, not simply to *test* the proof. We picked logic just because I happened to have *Principia Mathematica* sitting on my shelf and I was using it to see what was involved in finding a proof for anything." (*Principia Mathematica* is a classic book by Alfred North Whitehead and Bertrand Russell containing the theorems considered to form the foundations of mathematical logic. Russell was one of the first scientists to whom Simon wrote about LT in January 1956.)

And so LT was born, soon to be succeeded by General Problem Solver (GPS), which added another method of problem solving known as "means-ends analysis." Not only did these programs find proofs for theorems in the famous *Principia* but the proofs in some cases were based on previously undiscovered chains of logic. Many mathematicians even considered some of LT's proofs superior to those previously published.

The artificial intelligence of these programs, however, proved to be quite different from natural human intelligence. Although GPS could solve some problems considered to be quite difficult, it was unable to solve some that people consider easy. That pattern, as you will see, repeats itself throughout the history of AI: Computers excel in "difficult" tasks like chess, but teaching robots to see or to navigate successfully through an obstacle course has been difficult indeed!

IMITATION OR ENHANCEMENT?

"Mind tools," artificial intelligence programs such as expert systems and automatic reading systems, enhance a person's natural abilities. But Simon and Newell had a different purpose when they pioneered AI: to create a computer system that behaved in ways similar to a thinking brain. They could experiment with such a system and, by doing so, could improve our understanding of intelligence—human and otherwise. (Besides Simon and Newell, Professors John McCarthy and Marvin Minsky of the Massachusetts Institute of Technology are generally regarded as founders of AI for their pioneering work at about the same time. McCarthy later founded the artificial intelligence laboratory at Stanford University.)

"We're psychologists," Simon explains. "We were really much more interested in imitating [than enhancing]. We wanted to know how a system could be intelligent *even though* it could not try ten thousand things, *even though* it didn't have this large infallible memory."

Beyond that, Newell adds, "There is also the interest in just understanding the nature of intelligence itself, given that you believe that there can be other agents around besides humans. The larger question is [understanding] all possible ways of being intelligent, some of which are human; but you can imagine a number of other [kinds]." (The way that Newell uses the term *agent* here is common in computer science. It means anything that causes an action to occur in response to its analysis of a situation. An agent's analysis can be carried out in a human or animal wetware or in computer software.)

But although AI began as an imitation of intelligence, the idea of enhancement—mind tools—arose early in the field's history. As still happens today, the people working on AI sometimes divided into two camps, one interested in imitation and the other in enhancement. Sometimes one camp became critical of the other.

Newell remembers it this way:

You can see a very big separation in the field in its early days. Technical people disagreed with the whole direction in which artificial intelligence was moving. To them, the only proper use of the computer was to enhance and help people. But the people who were using computers for artificial intelligence were driven by the scientific urge to understand the nature of intelligent processes. They were not concerned with questions of how useful it was or whether you should start giving part of the task to a human and part of the task to a computer.

Where do Simon and Newell stand on the issue of imitation versus enhancement? A characteristic of

39

their work, "not shared by very much of the rest of the artificial intelligence field," says Newell, is to stand in both camps at the same time. "[We] always put together these two attitudes, not separating clearly when you're thinking about psychology and when you're thinking about computation. We believe that approach is, to use a phrase of Herbert's, one of our secret research weapons. It's where we get interesting places to discover new processes and new things that are going on. We look at it *both ways all the time.*"

Those are important words to remember. Just as many machines imitate the manipulations we perform with our bodies while enhancing our strength and agility, so do many mind tools mimic human information processing and augment it with superior computer capabilities. The best enhancement often begins with imitation.

5

From Information to Knowledge

We have described a computer as a PIPSY, a programmable information-processing system. But exactly what is information?

By *information*, we mean a fact or collection of facts. Information can take many forms, but if it is to be processed, it must be represented in a form that the information processor can understand. This paragraph, for example, represents information in a form that the human brain can process: a pattern of letters, punctuation marks, and blank space on a printed page.

Actually, before your brain can process what you read here, your eyes must see it (or your fingertips must feel it if you are reading Braille). The pattern of light and dark on the page of the book produces a similar pattern on the retinas of your eyes (or the pattern of bumps produces a pattern of pressure on your fingertips). That is then transformed into an electrical message—a pattern of signals—that travels along nerves to your brain.

Your brain has learned to interpret certain electrical patterns as written symbols, to interpret groups of symbols as words, groups of words as sentences, groups of sentences as paragraphs, and so forth. Ultimately the information in these paragraphs is processed—transformed—into information in a different form: chemical and physical changes in your brain. Reading actually produces changes in the chemical substances, the electrical signals, and the pattern of interconnections among neurons in your brain!

No matter what form the information takes, there is one common element: information is always represented as one kind of pattern or another.

BITS AND BYTES

Computers, like brains, process information in electrical form. Just as the brain needs eyes, a computer needs sensors to deal with input in another form, such as arrangements of letters on a page or patterns of magnetization on tapes or disks. The sensors transform those patterns into a series of on-off electrical signals, which the computer then processes. The processing results in a series of output signals from the computer. Those signals produce responses in other devices and parts of the computer itself.

Rather than thinking in terms of electrical signals, computer scientists usually deal with numbers or other symbols. They begin by representing "on" and "off" by the digits one and zero. For example, 11010001 stands for on-on-off-on-off-off-off-on.

Perhaps you have studied different number systems in school. If so, you might recognize that way of representing signals as the "base 2," or *binary*, number system. In our usual base 10, or *decimal*, number system, we use ten symbols called digits (0, 1, 2, 3, 4, 5, 6, 7, 8, and 9) to represent numbers. As you know, the value of the number depends not only on its digits but also on their order. That value is computed by reading the number's digits from right to left, multiplying each by its place value, and adding those products. The place value for the rightmost digit is one, and each place farther to the left has a place value ten times the previous one. Thus the value of 3047 is $(7 \times 1) + (4 \times 10) + (0 \times 100) + (3 \times 1000)$.

In the binary system, there are only two symbols, 0 and 1, and the place values double as you move leftward. Therefore, you can calculate that the binary number 11010001 has the same value as the decimal number 209: $(1 \times 1) + (0 \times 2) + (0 \times 4) + (0 \times 8) + (1 \times 16) + (0 \times 32) + (1 \times 64) + (1 \times 128) = 209$.

The basic unit of information for a computer, an on or an off signal, can therefore be considered a *binary digit,* or *bit* for short. You can use a string of binary digits to represent many things. For instance, you can do what computer scientists often do: group a certain number of bits together and view them as a unit. A common grouping is eight bits, which is often called a *byte.* If viewed as a number, a byte can have 256 different values, from 00000000 (0 in decimal numbers) through 11111111 (255 in decimal).

You might use those different bytes as a code. For instance, there are far fewer than 256 different symbols on a typewriter keyboard, even counting all uppercase (capital) and lowercase letters separately. So you could invent a code that represents each of those symbols by a different valued byte. In fact, when a computer stores a written document, it does so byte by byte, each byte standing for a letter, a digit, a punctuation mark, a space, a carriage return, or any other symbol the typist can type.

Sometimes, other ways of interpreting bits or bytes might be more useful. For instance, 10000010 01111111 10000010 00001000 10000010 00001000 11111110 00001000 10000010 00001000 10000010 00001000 10000010 01111111 might be a computer's way of saying hello on a video screen. The secret to interpreting this message is not to translate bytes into letters but rather to arrange the information in the following way:

Imagine that the video screen is divided into seven rows of sixteen squares. The message can fill the video screen, two bytes per row, if each square on the screen gets one bit of the message. Now imagine that a square is lit whenever its bit of the message is a 1 and dark whenever its bit is a 0. This is what you would see (where X is a bright spot and a period is a dark spot).

```
X . . . . X . . . X X X X X X X
X . . . . X . . . . . . X . . .
X . . . . X . . . . . . X . . .
X X X X X X . . . . . . X . . .
X . . . . X . . . . . . X . . .
X . . . . X . . . . . . X . . .
X . . . . X . . . X X X X X X X
```

Can you understand the message?

RELATIONSHIP AND MEANINGS

The meaning of the message becomes clear when you understand how the bytes are related. You don't look at them bit by bit or byte by byte but rather as a unit.

Once again, the information is contained in a pattern, and the way you interpret that pattern is determined by "programs" in your brain. Where did those programs come from? You created them yourself as you learned. First you learned the patterns of light and dark that made letters; then you learned the patterns of letters that made words. So although your eyes see 112 light and dark squares on the screen, your brain recognizes that the light squares form the word *HI* and understands that word as a common greeting in everyday English.

The meaning of that message depends not only on its information content—the bits that make it up—but also on the mind that perceives it. The mind interprets the message by looking for relationships among its bits and bytes. For a different message, where the information is more complicated, that mind is likely to organize the bytes or letters into words, the words into sentences, and the sentences into ideas. If the information is in the form of an image on the retina of an eye or the light-sensitive part of a camera, the mind may look for patterns and shapes that it recognizes as objects, then look for relationships among the objects, and finally develop a concept of the scene.

The ability to extract meaning from raw information requires intelligence. (If a computer can do that, some people would call it artificial intelligence.) If the information is new or unfamiliar, the mind's ability to give it meaning depends on what information that mind already has.

Think about how you deal with something new. During your life, you have developed ways of learning. You use very different techniques to learn different kinds of skills and ideas. But you always start out by trying to figure out where new information fits with what you already know. You look for relationships and connections among different pieces of information. You use those to build a structure of information, which you might call knowledge.

KNOWLEDGE ENGINEERING

When you are knowledgeable about a topic, you have found a way to build up an elaborate and efficient structure of information about that topic in your brain. That structure contains not only facts but also interconnections and relationships among the facts. No one knows exactly how people can build such structures in their brains, nor does anyone know what physical or chemical form those structures take. But no one doubts that the structures exist, and that the ability to build them—to connect facts and ideas—is an important ingredient of human intelligence.

Our lack of understanding of those structures in the brain is related to our lack of detailed knowledge of human wetware. Computers, however, are both less complicated and better understood than brains. Because a computer is a human creation, we know in complete detail how it processes information and in what form that information must be. We know exactly what structures in computers function as memory and what structures perform calculations.

The great value of computers as information processors is that they manipulate information far faster than humans can and do so with far greater precision and accuracy. (The distinction between precision and accuracy is this: *Precision* is a measure of the ability to distinguish between two items that are close to identical, but not exactly the same.

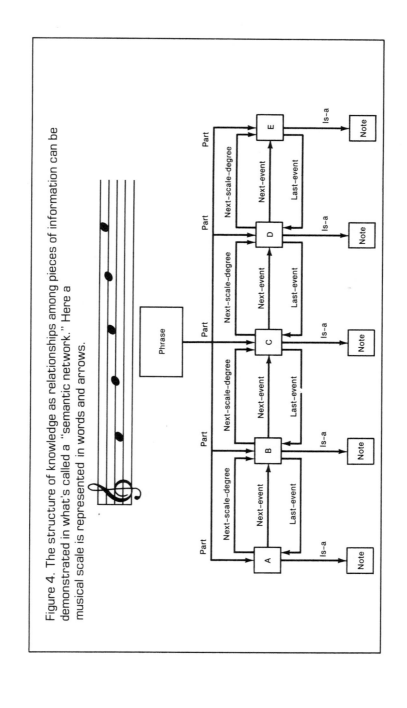

Figure 4. The structure of knowledge as relationships among pieces of information can be demonstrated in what's called a "semantic network." Here a musical scale is represented in words and arrows.

Accuracy is the ability to do the same thing every time. Humans are fallible and variable; computers follow their programs flawlessly.) They also have memories that store and recall information perfectly and in great detail. The great disadvantages of computers are that they are not nearly as good as humans at building and using knowledge nor at using incomplete or imprecise information. Most computer scientists believe that the day will come when computers overcome disadvantages. We just need to write better programs or build different kinds of machines.

But meanwhile, people are already building AI systems that take advantage of computers' better memory, speed, precision, and accuracy. These systems help us overcome our imperfections and make better use of our superior knowledge and superior ability to make connections among ideas.

Those AI systems rely on a field called *knowledge engineering*. Knowledge engineers use their understanding of hardware and software to develop an effective structure for a large amount of related information known as a data base. They have two important objectives: (1) to arrange the information in such a way that the computer can find facts quickly and (2) to enable the computer to develop, recognize, and use interrelationships among different parts of the data base (Figure 4).

6

Decision Making and Expert Systems

FROM KNOWLEDGE TO EXPERTISE

There is an old joke that an expert is someone who "knows more and more about less and less."

In most fields of knowledge (for example, paleontology, the study of fossils) the more you learn, the more interesting your questions become. Soon you find yourself asking—and answering—questions that no one has ever asked before. Suddenly, you know more and more about certain narrow areas of that field of knowledge (for example, the teeth of meat-eating dinosaurs) than anyone else, and you can apply your storehouse of knowledge to new questions, problems, or discoveries.

Following your special interest in that way leads you to become an expert. The "more and more" you know or can do is a special kind of knowledge or skill called "expertise"; the "less and less" is known as your "area of expertise." Expertise is often very scarce and valuable. The most specialized areas of expertise are usually the scarcest and most valuable.

It is fun to be an expert. Nearly everyone becomes an expert in some area. The nice part about human experts is that they are human as well as experts. But being human can also be a disadvantage. Computers are much better than people at making arithmetic calculations and sorting lists of information. Their memories store and retrieve information flawlessly. Human experts who use computers as mind tools can usually provide better advice than if they relied on their own limited and fallible memory and thinking power alone.

BUILDING AN EXPERT SYSTEM

Expertise is not just a collection of information. As you have just read, it is the ability to use specialized knowledge. Knowledge is organized information. To build expertise into a computer, therefore, you need, first, a way of organizing your information into knowledge and, second, a way to apply that knowledge. Taken together, the knowledge and the software to apply it expertly make up what is known as an *expert system* or, in some cases, a *decision-support system*.

Later in this chapter, you will read about particular expert and decision-support systems in areas of expertise such as medicine, mining, computer system design, automobile repair, music composition, and military missions. Some of those systems are well established; others are still experimental. To appreciate them fully, you need to know something about the main elements of an expert system and how they fit together. Those elements are (1) expert knowledge in a computer-usable form (facts), (2) ideas gained from experts' experience in using that knowledge (procedures), and (3) a computer program that uses that knowledge and experience to produce expert advice (Figure 5).

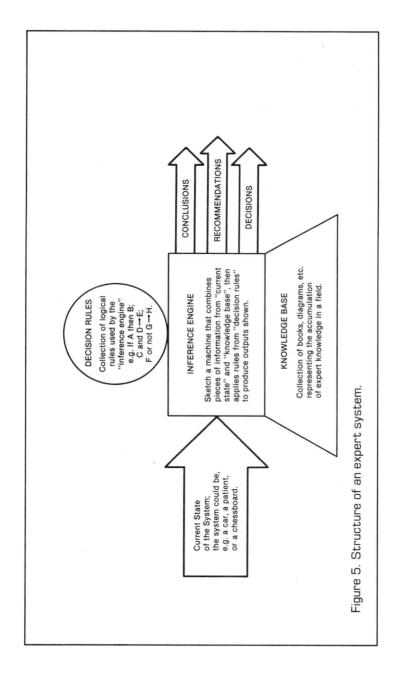

DECISION RULES

Collection of logical rules used by the "inference engine" e.g. If A then B; C and D→E; F or not G→H.

INFERENCE ENGINE

Sketch a machine that combines pieces of information from "current state" and "knowledge base", then applies rules from "decision rules" to produce outputs shown.

KNOWLEDGE BASE

Collection of books, diagrams, etc. representing the accumulation of expert knowledge in a field.

CONCLUSIONS

RECOMMENDATIONS

DECISIONS

Current State of the System; the system could be, e.g. a car, a patient, or a chessboard.

Figure 5. Structure of an expert system.

The Knowledge Base An expert or decision-support system is based on expert knowledge in the form of a data base called the *knowledge base*. Suppose you were a knowledge engineer setting out to build a knowledge base for a bridge-building expert system. You would begin by interviewing human experts who have designed bridges to learn what information they use and how they use it.

One of the first things you would discover is that they use engineering handbooks. One kind of handbook lists the physical properties of different materials under different conditions. Other handbooks describe components that might be used to build a bridge, such as the steel beams and cables. The designer needs to know the length and thickness of those beams and cables, what kinds of steel they are made of, where they are available, how long it takes to have them delivered, and what they cost.

Besides collecting all that information, you would also have to learn the mathematical equations that describe the relationships of the numbers in the handbooks and the important properties of a bridge or part of a bridge, such as strength or flexibility. Finally you would need to know what other factors the designer considers in building a bridge, such as the government regulations that have to be met; the reputations of the companies that make the steel, concrete, and other materials; the number of workers with particular skills needed for particular choices of design; and how long each part of the job takes.

The knowledge base is important because no one person can ever remember all those details and all their relationships. Your job as a knowledge engineer would be to organize that information in such a way that a person could instruct the computer to find the facts needed to make a decision quickly and correctly. The information also has to be organized so that the expert-system computer program can select and manipulate the information needed to perform the calculations that an expert designer does.

In addition, the information must be organized in such a way that it can be checked for correctness and consistency by both humans and computers. Finally, it must be organized so that new facts can be added, corrections or updates can be made, and out-of-date information can be removed.

So the job of a knowledge engineer is to design an organization for large quantities of diverse information. To do so requires expertise about the way computers work, the way humans think, and the way data bases can be built, structured, and manipulated.

Because it requires knowledge of so many different areas, knowledge engineering is a difficult job. If only we had a knowledge-engineering expert system, building a knowledge base would be a whole lot easier and more efficient! No doubt some AI researchers are already working toward that goal.

The Decision Rules Knowledge alone is not enough. If it were, then the person (or computer) with the best memory would always be the greatest expert. A very important part of expertise is the way the expert uses knowledge. In solving a problem or reaching a conclusion, an expert judges what facts are needed and gathers them together. Then the expert usually has a mental procedure to follow that produces the desired result.

That procedure often can be stated as a set of if-then *decision rules*. For example, in the design of bridges, there might be rule number 147, which states that if the bridge is over water that is deeper than 100 feet (30 meters) for a distance of more than 1 mile (1.6 kilometers), then you should design a suspension bridge. There might also be rule number 392: If the bridge is designed to carry trains, then its supports must all be made of a certain minimum grade of steel or better.

Some decision rules, like those examples in the last paragraph, are absolute. Others may be in the form of suggestions, recommendations, or advice. Some rules are based on analysis or scientific knowledge, but many are *heuristics* ("rules of thumb" based on experience). Expert systems may present the user with a single answer. But often they provide a set of suggested alternatives, leaving room for considerable human decision making. In that case, they are called *decision-support systems.*

If-then rules are often, but not always, the best way to capture expertise. When the number of alternatives is large and a great many facts are needed to make a decision, a different approach is usually used.

For instance, a physician often makes a medical diagnosis on the basis of how precisely a patient's symptoms match the usual pattern of symptoms of a particular disease or condition. Any single symptom could be associated with a large number of conditions, so the physician must gather a lot of information and draw on medical experience to diagnose the ailment and choose the course of treatment to follow.

In a medical expert or decision-support system, the heuristic knowledge of expert physicians is usually represented as a set of mathematical formulas. A physician who uses such a system is presented a number of alternative diagnoses and treatments.

Each alternative has a numerical score or an indication of likelihood (for example, highly likely, probable, possible, unlikely, ruled out).

If-then rules provide one very great advantage over heuristic formulas: When a user wants to understand the reason behind a recommendation, the program can simply list the rules that it used. A heuristic system can also have that capability, but only to a limited extent.

The Inference Engine An expert system provides its recommendation by applying all of its if-then rules all at once. A computer program called an *inference engine* runs and compares the "if" clause, or the *hypothesis,* of the rule to the situation at hand. Whenever the hypothesis of the rule is true (or "satisfied"), then the "then" clause, or the *conclusion,* is also true, and the rule is said to be "activated." (The inference engine gets its name because a human acting in the same way as the program would infer that the conclusion is true from the knowledge that the hypothesis is true.)

For example, if you are designing a railroad bridge, then every rule that begins, "If the bridge is to carry trains," is activated. In that case, the expert system does not permit you to select a grade of steel inferior to that specified by rule 392. If you do try to select a cable of a lesser grade, the system may even quote rule 392 to explain what you are doing wrong.

An interesting property of the inference engine is that it would operate in the same way whether the area of expertise were bridge construction, computer system design, mineral exploration, or creation of a knowledge base. It behaves like a judge who carries out the law, no matter what the law is.

In theory, then, one inference engine would be all anyone would need; each application would have its own knowledge base and decision rules, but the actual decision making would be handled by the same judge. That would be a significant advantage over creating a program based on heuristic formulas, which would then require a different judge for each application.

But in practice, each inference engine that has ever been written has its own sets of strengths and weaknesses. Each has been designed to take advantage of the particular structure of certain knowledge bases and sets of decision rules.

Another practical consideration is that each decision rule has to be tested at each stage of the decision-making process. Large sets of rules are cumbersome to work with and slow to produce their recommendations. No inference engine today can handle more than a few thousand rules and still provide useful expert advice quickly enough. If you need more than that number of rules for your application, then you have to use heuristic formulas.

Some advanced inference engines and knowledge-base organizations avoid testing all the rules at every step. They also can test several rules at once. A system called Soar at Carnegie-Mellon University can make decisions based on 10,000 rules at the rate of about one decision per second and does not slow down appreciably as more rules are added.

The Soar approach mimics the way a human expert brings a great deal of expertise to bear on a decision in a short time. In that sense, it is simililar to using a single mathematical formula to represent heuristic knowledge instead of using many rules to represent the same thing.

EXAMPLES OF EXPERT AND DECISION-SUPPORT SYSTEMS

Now let's look at how some real expert and decision-support systems work. We'll start with two from the medical field.

CADUCEUS, a Medical Decision-Support System In the early 1980s, Dr. Jack D. Myers, a specialist in internal medicine at the University of Pittsburgh, and Dr. Harry E. Pople, a professor in that university's School of Business, developed a heuristic decision-support system called INTERNIST-1. It was made up of a computer program and a collection of about 100,000 numbers based on Dr. Myers's forty years of medical experience.

In the program were formulas, devised by Dr. Pople on the basis of his knowledge of mathematics and statistics, which used those numbers and facts about the patient to compute scores for each of more than 500 diseases. The program then used the scores either to suggest a diagnosis or to ask the physician for more information about the patient.

INTERNIST-1 was as accurate as many physicians in diagnosing illnesses in internal medicine, but not as good as Dr. Myers. That's typical of a decision-support system. It is better than many intelligent and knowledgeable people because it never forgets a large body of information. But even the best computer scientists can't write programs that organize and use that information as well as human experts.

Many physicians who tried INTERNIST-1 called it "Jack-in-the-box" because it often seemed to think just like Dr. Myers. But Drs. Pople and Myers didn't agree. They knew that they could make it give even better answers, especially in a few important situations when it just wasn't very helpful. So they and several colleagues developed and are still improving CADUCEUS, a decision-support system that improves on the best ideas from INTERNIST-1 and combines them with computer data on the care of individual hospital patients.

CADUCEUS does not pop up with a diagnosis as "Jack-in-the-box" did. Rather, it operates as a computerized medical chart that guides a skilled physician to provide the best overall care for each patient.

MYCIN, an Expert System for Diagnosing Infection At about the same time that Pople and Myers began work on INTERNIST in Pittsburgh, a group at Stanford University, led by Professors Edward Feigenbaum and Bruce Buchanan, began to develop a computer technique to diagnose infectious diseases and to suggest a course of treatment. They called their program MYCIN since many infection-treating antibiotic medicines have names that end in the suffix -mycin.

Nine researchers including Buchanan decided to put MYCIN to the test. A particularly complex disease to treat is meningitis, a dangerous inflammation of the membrane surrounding the spinal cord. It can result from an infection by any of several viruses, fungi (plural of *fungus)*, or bacteria (including the rod-shaped organism that causes tuberculosis). The different forms of meningitis have many of the same symptoms, but they respond differently to different courses of treatment.

The research team looked at ten meningitis patients and gave the same information to MYCIN, to a Stanford faculty member specializing in infectious diseases, to a resident (a physician who is studying to become a specialist in a field of medicine by working with an expert in that area), and to a medical student. MYCIN, the two doctors, and the student each made a diagnosis and recommended treatment for each of the patients.

After the patients recovered, a team of evaluators compared the actual treatment and course of the disease for each patient to the diagnoses and recommendations produced by MYCIN and the three humans. The evaluators were impartial judges since they did not know who or what had made which diagnosis and recommendation. Their conclusion was that MYCIN's diagnoses and recommendations were at least as good as any of the others!

MYCIN was significant in two ways. First, because the area of expertise for MYCIN was narrow enough to apply if-then rules rather than heuristics, Feigenbaum and Buchanan were led to the idea of separating the knowledge base from the inference engine. Second, the success of MYCIN, reported in the *Journal of the American Medical Association* in 1979, was so spectacular that it launched the expert-system industry. More than a decade later, the industry is still thriving and growing. Many small expert-system companies have sprung up and many major companies have built their own very successful expert systems.

SBDS, the Automobile Service Bay Diagnostic System If expert systems can be used for diagnosing and recommending treatment of desperately ill meningitis victims, then expert systems should certainly be useful in the diagnosis and treatment of "sick" cars. That is the idea behind SBDS, the Automobile Service Bay Diagnostic System.

Automotive diagnosticians are not ordinary car-repair people. Their time is often in such demand that they only diagnose problems and suggest repairs, leaving the manual work to others. Their expertise is so rare that not every repair shop can afford one. Furthermore, diagnosticians get sick and take vacations, and some days they are not at their best. SBDS makes it possible for a repair shop to have a computerized version of an expert diagnostician on call at all times.

The Carnegie Group, an expert-system company located in Pittsburgh, developed SBDS in cooperation with the Ford Motor Company and Hewlett-Packard Company. The Carnegie Group's knowledge engineers worked with Ford's best automotive diagnosticians to capture their expertise in the SBDS knowledge base. They also worked with Hewlett-Packard to develop a SBDS computer system inexpensive enough to be put in nearly every service department for cars made by Ford.

That computer system runs a program that interacts with mechanics, who do not need specialized training in computers. The program uses an inference engine and the SBDS diagnostic knowledge base. It asks the mechanics questions and gives them advice (Figure 6). As Ford products change, updated SBDS knowledge bases will replace older ones.

The developers believe that their system will transform each SBDS service department so that it will seem as if Ford's best automobile diagnostician works there, every minute of every day, not even taking time off for lunch.

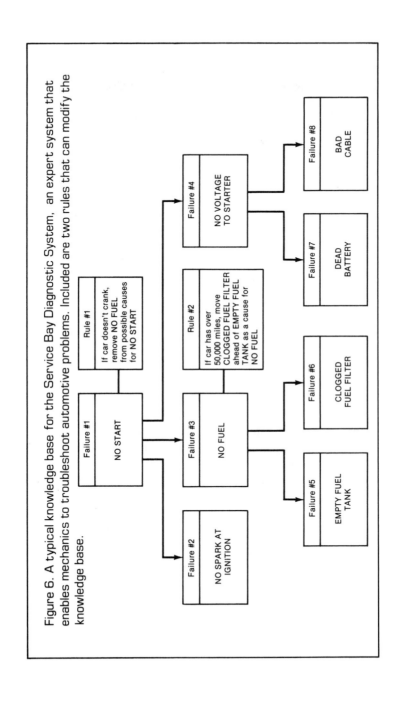

Figure 6. A typical knowledge base for the Service Bay Diagnostic System, an expert system that enables mechanics to troubleshoot automotive problems. Included are two rules that can modify the knowledge base.

AI Systems for Music Composition Even when people are at their most creative, a lot of what they do is routine. For example, music is generally thought of as one of humanity's most creative activities, and composition is one of the most creative parts of music. Yet composition contains many routine elements, and AI systems have been created to assist with them.

A composer, for example, may write a repeating pattern of timpani (kettledrum) music that carries through a long segment of a piece, accompanying the other instruments, which are carrying the main theme. Or a musical phrase may repeat frequently throughout a piece, appearing transposed into another key, in another octave, or written for different instruments. How much simpler it is to be able to compose on a system that automatically produces those parts of the musical score. And how much more of a composer's time can be devoted to the more original elements.

For the study of music composition, it is possible to capture, in knowledge bases, particular musical concepts or the elements that define a certain style, such as a certain dance; the folk music of a particular ethnic group; or the characteristic orchestrations, tonalities, and rhythms of a particular composer. There are even programs that compose their own music (Figure 7).

Why do many people consider computer tools of this sort to be expert systems instead of other forms of AI (or simply computer aids)? Because they believe that the programs enable people with moderate musical talent to enhance their ideas with expert musicianship.

Other Expert Systems The expert-system area is growing so fast that it is impossible to cover all the areas in which it applies. Here are a few that should be mentioned:

- Prospector, an expert system for mineral exploration.

- Expert and decision-support systems for national defense, such as Pilot's Associate which can take over routine flight tasks so fighter pilots can concentrate on carrying out their high-speed missions.

- Computer-system design by expert systems such as Digital Equipment Corporation's pioneering program XCON.

- Financial decisions, from investing in new products to buying or selling stocks to deciding whether to approve a loan.

- Construction, including a system to design prefabricated houses

- Layout of printed materials from newspapers to Yellow Pages telephone directories.

The great British mathematician Alan Turing
played a key role in the development of early
computers. He also formulated the
now-famous Turing test of machine
intelligence, which states that if a computer
can make you think it is human, then
it is a "thinking machine."

Above: A model of the difference engine,
designed in 1821 by Charles Babbage
to compute large navigational
and astronomical tables

Facing page: Lady Ada Lovelace was the
world's first computer programmer
and probably the first person to consider
the question, "Can computers think?"

Three pioneers of artificial intelligence:
Herbert Simon (above) and Alan Newell
(facing page, top), both of
Carnegie-Mellon University, and
Marvin Minsky (right) of the
Massachusetts Institute of Technology

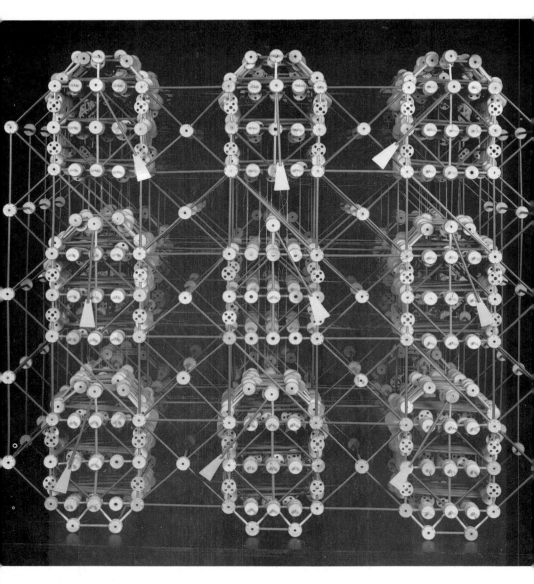

This tinkertoy mechanical computer can flawlessly play ticktacktoe. Such a machine demonstrates that intelligent systems need not be based on digital electronics.

One-time world-champion correspondence
chess player Hans Berliner led the
development of the hardware and software
for HiTech, one of the best chess-playing
machines in the world. He also
created a backgammon program that
defeated the world backgammon
champion in a challenge match.

Brian Marsh of the University of Rochester plays checkers against a robot. Marsh wrote the computer checker program. The robot has sophisticated vision capabilities that enable it to distinguish between red and black checkers, and then grasp the checkers to move and jump.

Charles Ames created the
Cybernetic Composer program, an
artificial intelligence
software system that composes
music in a variety of styles.

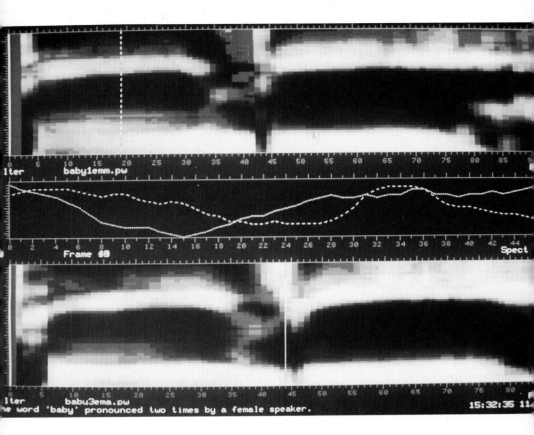

Text visible within the image:

0 5 10 15 20 25 30 35 40 45 50 55 60 65 70 75 80 85 9
lter baby1emm.pw

0 2 4 6 8 10 12 14 16 18 20 22 24 26 28 30 32 34 36 38 40 42 44
Frame 48   Spect

5 10 15 20 25 30 35 40 45 50 55 60 65 70 75 80
lter baby3ema.pw
he word 'baby' pronounced two times by a female speaker.   15:32:35 11

Left: Dr. Tim Binford of the robotics
lab at Stanford University developed an
AI-based aircraft recognition system.

Above: Voiceprints can aid in giving a computer
"ears." Here the monitor of a speech
analyzer displays two pronunciations
of the word "baby" as horizontal bands.
Note the difference in appearance.

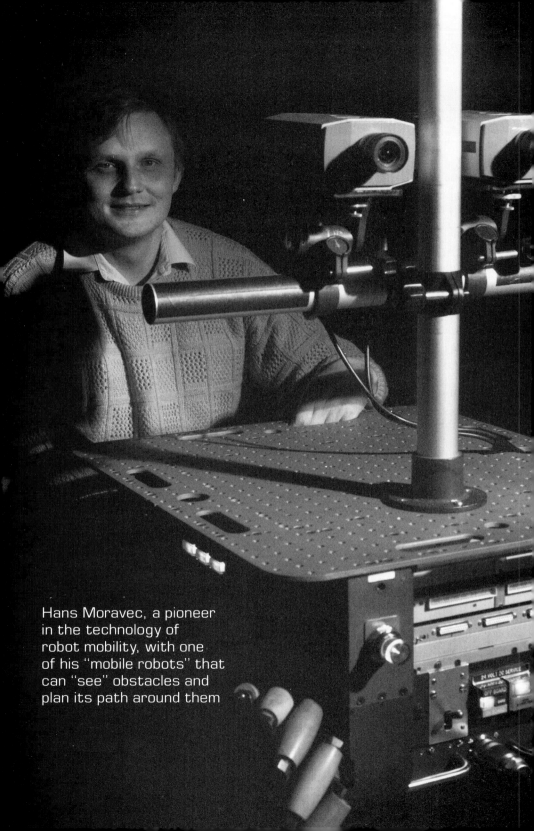

Hans Moravec, a pioneer in the technology of robot mobility, with one of his "mobile robots" that can "see" obstacles and plan its path around them

One of Moravec's early robots, the
"Stanford Cart," enjoys a stroll in
the California sun. One of the
difficulties in the development of
such "computer vision" robots was
that they sometimes perceived shadows
to be solid objects and were also
fooled by shadows that moved
during the several minutes needed
to compute each robot step.

A blind person uses the Kurzweil Reading Machine. This machine uses optical character recognition (OCR) to scan text. It then converts the symbols on the page into synthesized speech.

A speech recognition system:
when the child says the correct
word, the bear smiles.

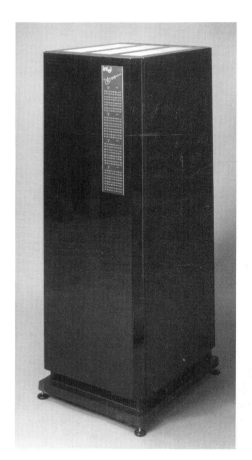

Many artificial intelligence applications require the enormous computing power of supercomputers. Shown left is an Intel Corporation supercomputer, the brains of which are the four square microprocessors on 9″ × 11″ boards (below). Each microprocessor contains its own memory.

7

Computers That Play Chess

The rules of most board or card games are simple, clear, and easy to explain. These characteristics make them, in a sense, completely predictable and analyzable. Yet their simple rules permit an enormous number of possible combinations of moves and countermoves—so many combinations, in fact, that no human mind can describe or analyze all possible contests.

This mind-challenging complexity that arises from simple rules fascinates analytical game players. The way people respond to that complexity makes certain games enormously interesting to scientists who study human and machine intelligence.

Hans J. Berliner of Carnegie-Mellon University is one such scientist. In the June 1980 issue of *Scientific American*, Berliner describes how his computer program beat the world backgammon champion in a challenge match in Monte Carlo.

That article succeeds in teaching the rules of the game in only a few paragraphs, showing how simple it is to learn. At the same time, Berliner also demonstrates the challenge of learning to play backgammon well.

Berliner was able to capture hard-won human

backgammon expertise in the form of heuristics in a computer program. Then by putting the program through many trial games and analyzing its play, he refined the program until it could play at world-championship level.

Some people might argue that the success of Berliner's program means that playing backgammon doesn't require great intelligence. But there is another way to look at it: Given expertise, a computer can use its large infallible memory and rapid computation skill to outperform a human mind. The challenge is to give the computer that expertise.

That's what Berliner did. He did not capture the full extent of the backgammon expertise available to him (it is unlikely that anyone could do that), but he captured a lot. Most importantly, he combined the expertise with the computer's superhuman memory and computational ability. The result was an outstanding electronic backgammon player.

CHESS-PLAYING COMPUTERS

The rules of chess are more complicated than those of backgammon, but they are still easy to write in a computer program. In chess as in backgammon, the challenge for artificial intelligence researchers is to capture chess-playing expertise.

Chess playing has long been regarded as one of the most demanding forms of intellectual exercise. It involves the ability to envision two-dimensional patterns, to coordinate an array of different pieces that move according to different rules, to plan a series of moves that will trap (checkmate) your opponent's king, and to deduce and foil your opponent's plan to trap yours. Unlike backgammon, which always ends in a victory, chess frequently ends in a draw.

Competitive chess playing is well developed throughout the world. An enormous amount is written about the game: columns about chess in regular newspapers and magazines; specialty newspapers and magazines devoted entirely to chess; and books on chess history, chess strategy, great chess matches and players, and even particular styles of play.

Chess organizations such as the United States Chess Federation (USCF) rank their member players by a complicated scoring system based on their records in games against opponents of various ratings. An *expert* has a USCF rating between 2000 and 2200. To be a *master* requires a rating of between 2200 and 2400. Above that are the few hundred very best players in the world, called *senior masters* and *grand masters*. The current world champion, Gary Kasparov, has achieved a rating of approximately 2800.

Beyond the intellectual challenge, research in computer chess seeks to answer some fundamental questions in artificial intelligence, such as the relative importance of "brute force" (computer speed and memory size) and knowledge (including knowledge engineering). The noted computer scientist Edward Fredkin believes so strongly in the intellectual and practical benefits to be gained from computer chess research that he has offered a $100,000 prize to the person or team who develops a computer that defeats the world champion in an official match of at least twelve games.

Chess-Playing Programs A very important element of the program in a chess-playing machine is the move generator. Given the present board position, the move generator determines the new board position for every possible legal move. For each of those positions, it can compute every legal countermove and the positions that will result from them.

If the program could run long enough, the move generator could compute all possible countercountermoves, countercountercountermoves, and so forth, until it reached a move that would end the game. In that event, it might find one or more moves that would guarantee victory after a long series of moves no matter how the opponent responded. If that would happen, then chess would be considered a "solved problem," and the move generator would be nearly the whole program.

But no one expects that to happen because the program simply could not run long enough. Furthermore, there is not enough material in the universe to build a computer memory large enough to store all the possible move-countermove sequences to test whether any one of the twenty possible opening moves is guaranteed to produce victory.

Herbert Simon estimates that there are about as many possible different move sequences in chess as there are molecules in the universe—ruling out building a memory to store them all. At 1000 times the current speed of the very best chess-playing machines, it would take more than 40 billion years (more than twice the age of the universe) to compute them!

And then it would need nearly another 40 billion years to compute the second move. (Current machines would need 40 trillion years!)

So the move generator alone is not enough. To play chess in a reasonable amount of time (tournament chess rules limit the total time the players have for their moves), the computer program must be selective in the moves it considers. For example, it may generate all possible positions resulting from a "search depth" of six moves, three by each player. This would take the current fastest chess-playing computer a few seconds at the beginning of a game.

Unless the computer is nearing a win, these six-move-later positions will not reveal a clear victory. Thus the program normally needs another way to evaluate which move is best. A human chess expert can look at a chess board and evaluate the strength of the position for either player. The computer program needs a similar "evaluator" based on human expertise and experience.

A human expert's evaluation begins with counting the "material"—the pieces remaining on the board for each side—scoring one point for each pawn, three points for each bishop or knight, five points for each rook, and nine points for each queen. The computer program's evaluator starts in the same way.

Next the expert considers the value of the position of each piece and combination of pieces—upgrading the evaluation if the piece or pieces control the center of the board, downgrading the value of a piece that is temporarily blocked from moving, and so forth. Chess-playing computer programs' evaluators also do this.

As chess machines have developed, their programmers have learned to write more sophisticated evaluators. Often the improvements in the evaluators are made in response to moves that human players would recognize as blunders: mistakes that result from a "blind spot" in the heuristic formulas. In many cases, these blind spots permit the computer's opponent to sneak in a long-term strategy with results that do not become apparent to the computer program until after more moves than its current search depth.

Some chess-playing programs prevent those blunders not only by refining the evaluator but also by using a technique known as *singular extension*. In that case, when a single move or a few moves look particularly promising, the program increases its search depth for those moves only, often searching many moves ahead to look for pitfalls.

Brute Force versus Knowledge Chess experts draw on three forms of expertise: (1) their knowledge of the chess literature, (2) their ability to evaluate positions, and (3) their ability to plan. People developing chess-playing computer systems build expertise on the same three elements.

Chess-playing computers have advantages and disadvantages when compared to their human counterparts. These are similar to the advantages and disadvantages of expert and decision-support systems. For example, expert and decision-support systems take advantage of a computer's large, infallible memory. But their rules or heuristics do not capture human expertise perfectly.

Let's compare human and electronic chess players by looking at the three elements of chess expertise.

Knowledge of the Chess Literature
There are two important aspects of knowing the chess literature. We'll call them "bags of tricks" and "classic games."

Expert human chess players have quite versatile bags of tricks, many of which they have learned by reading the chess literature. They remember opening sequences, strong sequences of moves at other times of the game, ways in which certain combinations of pieces can be most effective, and strategies (guiding concepts for offense and defense that produce a particular style of play).

Those experts also remember certain classic games, especially those in which a particularly creative and surprising move led to victory or thwarted the opponent's plan. The strength of such a move is usually clear immediately after it is made, but most players—even very strong ones—would have overlooked it because their thinking was focused on other possibilities.

Knowledge of classic games adds new tricks to experts' bags or protects them in unusual situations when their usual tricks would lead them astray.

Since computer memories are more reliable than human ones, you might think that electronic chess players would have a knowledge advantage over expert human players. Human chess players, however, have two advantages over computers in this area. First, their brains are magnificent knowledge engineers. The literature that they remember is organized in ways that are well matched to the way they personally view chess. Second, they constantly compare the present game situation to their knowledge base. When they recognize similarities between the present board position and situations in the literature, they can pull their next move from their bag of tricks or their memory storehouse of classic games.

Computer programs rarely do that because programmers have not found a way to incorporate human recognition of *similarity*. So except for a few opening sequences, most chess-playing computers are unable to use knowledge of the chess literature effectively. Programmers of AI chess machines have therefore decided that they can be more effective by applying the computer's power to techniques like singular extension rather than struggling to find ways of comparing board positions with a chess-literature data base.

Evaluation

Chess-playing programs use heuristic formulas rather than if-then rules to evaluate each board position. Although these evaluators are becoming more sophisticated as AI researchers gain experience with chess-playing machines, they do have their blind spots.

Since humans can't always describe the heuristics they use to evaluate a given board position, it is impossible for AI programmers to capture this element of human expertise perfectly. Thus humans have a significant advantage over computers in evaluating a particular position.

However, computers have two advantages over humans that partially offset this. First, their speed in calculating enables computers to evaluate many more positions than a human can consider. Second, the computer will perform an evaluation calculation correctly every time. Even the best human players are not so dependable. They sometimes overlook something that they would normally notice, making their evaluation dangerously incorrect and leading to a blunder.

Planning

Once a human chess player has decided on a strategy, he or she next develops tactics: moves that will carry it out. Chess players know that their human opponents, like them, have strategies and are planning tactics. As the game unfolds, each player's tactics change as the other's strategy is revealed.

At any point during the play, the players have

plans based on their own tactics and their opponent's expected responses. Both players are looking ahead several moves; how far ahead depends on their skill level.

In studying chess and in developing chess-playing computers, AI experts agree that the ability to look ahead is crucial, but they argue about how many moves ahead chess grandmasters see. The grand masters can't settle the argument because they describe their plans in terms of expected changes in the board position, not move by move.

In looking ahead, the grand masters can't possibly consider every possible move-countermove sequence: there are simply too many for a human mind to handle. Instead they concentrate on the most plausible moves. They may even perform a human kind of singular extension, looking far down the most promising path many moves into the future. The difference between human singular extension and computer singular extension is that the human thought process is guided by the player's strategy and the presumed strategy of the opponent.

Computer chess programs are not designed to have strategies. The computer's planning is generally guided by looking at all possible board positions as far into the future as possible, then selecting the most promising move, assuming that the opponent plays as well as possible.

To a human playing against the computer, the machine may seem to have a strategy and to be planning. But it is not. The machine is simply carrying out a "brute-force" search, using all of its computational power. It was programmed to win simply by looking farther into the future than a human opponent. This greater look-ahead makes it likely to choose a better move than the human one, even though it has a less sophisticated evaluator and no strategy at all.

The computer seems to be planning because (1) its program has considered moves far into the future and (2) its evaluator is good enough so that it usually makes the same choices that a human expert would.

THE QUEST FOR THE FREDKIN PRIZE

In the early years of AI, a favorite topic of researchers' speculation was whether a computer would ever be able to beat the world chess champion. Herbert Simon and Allen Newell, two of AI's founders, had no doubts. In 1958, they predicted that the best chess player in the world in 1968 would be a computer.

Although they may have underestimated the world champion's level of skill and therefore the number of years until their prediction would come true, Simon and Newell's key idea, that a computer would be able to play world-class chess within the foreseeable future, has been proved correct. People no longer ask *whether* a computer will beat the world chess champion, but *when*.

Edward Fredkin offered a $100,000 prize to speed up the process. He also offered two intermediate prizes: $5,000 to the people behind the first computer program to achieve a master rating and $10,000 to the people whose computer competes at the grandmaster level.

Those intermediate prizes have already been claimed. The first award went to Ken Thompson, whose program, "Belle," reached the 2200 level in 1982. The second intermediate Fredkin Award went to Feng-Hsiung Hsu, Murray Campbell, and Thomas

Anantharaman, who built and programmed "Deep Thought," a computer specially designed for speed in playing chess. It analyzes 1 million board positions per second!

The Deep Thought team built their machine while studying at Carnegie-Mellon University and improved it at the IBM Corporation, where they are now employed. Deep Thought achieved its grandmaster rating in 1989 and is now the favorite in the race for Fredkin's $100,000 prize.

In New York City on October 22, 1989, with the non-chess-player Hsu moving the pieces, Deep Thought played a two-game match against World Champion Kasparov. The champion prevailed, but he knew he had faced a worthy opponent.

The next time Hsu sits across a chessboard from Kasparov, Deep Thought will be even better. Hsu and his colleagues are redesigning its evaluator to make it even smarter and replacing its two computer "chips" with a single one—five times faster. Campbell, the chess expert of the team, expects the improvements to bring DT to the 2800–2900 level, enough to make Kasparov worry about losing.

And as if that weren't enough, IBM plans to spend $300,000 to design a newer machine with 1000 interconnected chess chips. That machine, which will probably be given a new name, is expected to be able to analyze *1 billion* positions per second and to achieve a USCF rating of 3500. If that estimate is correct, the new machine should be able to beat any human champion so decisively that the match would be boring.

8

Computer Vision and Hearing

Among the most interesting applications of artificial intelligence are those which enable robots to interact with their environment. Just as humans have *senses* that enable them to see, hear, smell, and feel, robots have input devices called *sensors* that give them similar abilities. And just as humans use their senses as well as their bodies when they move from place to place, mobile robots are designed to use information from their sensors as they find their way.

Sensors can give robots and computers the ability to respond to many different aspects of their environment. This chapter concentrates on the two most well-developed humanlike senses: computer vision and hearing.

BRAINS THAT SEE

Look at the room around you, and imagine that you have been sent on a mission to walk through the nearest doorway and to call out the name of every obstacle you encounter on the way out. Before you start to move, you plan your path, taking into account that you will have to walk around some things and step over others.

77

After taking a few steps, it would not surprise you to notice an obstacle that you didn't see at first. The new obstacle would force you to change your plan. This might happen several times, but you would eventually reach the door.

Now think of a slightly different task. You are placed in the same familiar room, but you are blindfolded and told to use a cane or your hands to feel for obstacles. Now it is harder to get out of the room because your mental picture of your surroundings is not perfect. But still you find your way out.

Getting out of the room takes intelligence. If you were asked what is the hardest part of the task for you without the blindfold, it would probably be planning your path. With the blindfold, it would probably be naming the obstacles you discover on the way.

If a robot had to do the same task, it would have to use artificial intelligence. Suppose that you had a robot equipped with top-quality television cameras on rotating platforms for seeing clearly in any direction, versatile jointed legs for walking, a knowledge base containing images of thousands of objects, and a supercomputer. What part of the task would be the most difficult for the robot?

Surprisingly, it might be recognizing the closest door! A careful look at human and robot vision will help you understand why that is so.

When you see something, your brain really does the seeing; your eyes are merely cameralike sensors used as input devices. Each eye has a lens that focuses light onto an area called the *retina*. The retina is made up of cells that respond to the light by sending electrical signals along the optic nerve to the brain.

When a robot "sees" something, it uses television as the sensor. If a robot uses the best available

TV cameras, the images produced by its eyes can be nearly as sharp as the images on a human retina. And in some ways, robot TV eyes can be far better than ours.

For example, a robot could see on the darkest of nights using a detector of the invisible infrared radiation that is given off by all warm objects. Or a robot could have as many eyes as its designer decided. These eyes could be anywhere, even far from the robot's body, and could look in any direction.

If sight were based on sensors alone, robots could see better than we humans do. But seeing is not just producing an image: it is also recognizing patterns in the image. Looking at it another way, seeing is not only gathering information from input devices, but recognizing patterns and relationships in that information. Seeing requires intelligence and a knowledge base!

We usually recognize each object in a scene, seemingly in an instant and without effort. Yet even if the robot's knowledge base contains an image of each object in a scene, its computer brain requires great effort to identify these objects, and it may fail to recognize many of them. Clearly, this is a case where human wetware is vastly superior to the best hardware and software available.

Let's look at some of the difficulties a computer-vision system has to face. In doing so, we will gain insight into the functioning of the mental part of a human vision system.

FINDING AN OBJECT

You probably have had some experiences that can help you to understand how much intelligence is

79

needed to see an object. For example, you may have seen drawings or photographs with a challenge to find "hidden" objects.

Think about trying to spot a white calf with black spots standing on a snowy, rock-strewn hillside. The outline of the calf's body against the background of snow is hard to notice, especially since its black spots look like rocks sticking out of the blanket of snow. When you finally find the animal, it is probably because you notice the pattern of its facial features or the distinctive shape of a hoof.

The reason you have trouble seeing the calf is that your brain identifies objects by seeking contrasts in the retinal images. The contrasts between the spots and the calf's body look almost the same as the contrasts between the rocks and the snow. Meanwhile, there is little contrast between the calf's body and the snow. So your brain focuses on the calf's spots instead of the calf.

You can overcome that problem with conscious effort, but it isn't automatic. That's the first problem computer vision systems have to face: what is an object?

HV (HUMAN VISION) AND TV

Signals and Pixels The part of your brain called the *visual cortex* has a structure that makes it sensitive to contrasts in the electrical signals that reach it from the retina. As far as researchers can tell, there are many similarities between those retinal signals and TV camera signals.

A television picture can be thought of as an array of little rectangular picture elements, or *pixels*, arranged in horizontal lines. The camera scans the scene before it, line by line throughout the picture, thirty times every second in North America (twenty-five times per second in most of the rest of the world). That rate is fast enough so that the human vision system interprets it as a moving picture, not the series of still images that it really is.

If the picture is black and white, the brightness of each pixel determines the shade of gray at that spot. If the picture is in color, it is actually a composite of three separate images in three different colors.

To process a TV picture by computer, the electrical signal must be turned into bits. That is easily done. Each scan line of the image is produced by a varying electrical signal as a beam crosses the screen. To convert that into bits, the average intensity of that signal as it crosses each pixel is represented by a certain number of bits, depending on how fine a gray scale is desired. Six bits is enough to produce 64 different shades from full dark to full brightness.

The number of pixels per row and the number of rows per picture can vary. Standard television now has 525 lines per picture, but high-definition television (HDTV) with more than twice that number of lines for a sharper image will soon be common. If each line of the HDTV image contained as many pixels as there were lines in the picture, then the image would have more than a million pixels altogether. One color picture would require more than 10 million bits. So a normal-speed HDTV signal would contain more than 300 million bits of information per second!

The main difference between human vision and television is in the scanning. The information in a television signal is a series of numbers, representing the pixels in the order in which they are scanned.

Information transferred in this way is called *serial* or *sequential*. The human retina is made up of an array of light-sensitive cells, each of which is connected to the optic nerve. Each cell produces a series of electrical impulses much like the pixels in a TV signal, but the impulses from all the cells travel along the nerve at the same time. This is called *parallel* transfer of information.

Detecting Edges and Corners A computer-vision system compares the numbers of each pixel to those nearby. The computer is programmed to pay more attention to areas of high contrast, that is, pixels in which the numbers are changing sharply over a short distance. The programs interpret regions of contrast as edges and corners that form the boundaries of objects.

Having detected what appears to be an object (although it may only be a high-contrast region within an object, such as a black spot on a white calf), many computer-vision programs then carry out procedures designed to recognize that object. (A few computer-vision programs, such as those designed to guide a welding robot, are simpler, needing only to recognize edges.)

To identify the object it has detected, the computer-vision program compares the shape of the boundary with shapes of known objects in its knowledge base. If the match is close enough, the program has "recognized" something.

How close is "close enough"? That depends on how the vision system is being used. If the objects are always the same distance from the lens, then the match may require size as well as shape matching.

The most important computer-vision application

that requires the ability to recognize alternate forms is optical character recognition. Hand-written and printed letters and numbers vary greatly in shape and size, but there are essential features that enable a computer-vision system to read them, at least in limited circumstances.

APPLICATIONS OF OPTICAL CHARACTER RECOGNITION

Two innovations in optical character recognition have had major benefits for large groups of people. The first of these is the Kurzweil Reading Machine (KRM). This machine combines optical recognition of printed characters with a speech synthesizer and AI pronunciation rules. The result is a device that enables a blind person to scan a page printed in English and listen to the machine read the words. The KRM was introduced in 1976, and many improvements have been made since. With it, a blind person has access to most written documents instead of just the few published in Braille or audio form.

Two years after his KRM, Kurzweil introduced the Kurzweil Data Entry Machine, which uses optical character recognition to transfer information directly from the printed page to a computer data file.

The second major innovation is speeding mail delivery in the United States. Beginning in 1990, the U.S. Postal Service began encouraging people to address their letters with a new format suitable for use with their new machines. When a properly addressed letter passes through the post office's optical character recognition system, it finds and reads the zip code. Then it prints a bar code version

Obstacles to Recognition

So far, except for the calf in the snow and similar unusual cases, it does not seem too difficult for a computer program to identify objects in television pictures. But that is far from the truth. There are many factors that human wetware deals with easily—seemingly automatically—that turn out to be too complicated to implement in hardware and software.

• **Rotation** You have little difficulty recognizing an object in an image, even if it is upside-down, sideways, or at an angle. To produce that ability in a computer requires special hardware or software. Many factory assembly robots with vision systems avoid the rotation problem by relying on mechanisms that always present the objects to the robot in one of a small number of predictable alignments.

• **2-D Images of a 3-D World** The lenses of our eyes produce two-dimensional images on our retinas, from which our brains produce a three-dimensional mental picture. Most people can recognize a car from practically any angle, even from underneath. But think of how different it is for a computer analyzing a television picture of that same car. The pattern of edges and corners that the computer "sees" is vastly different when the car is photographed from different locations and directions.

• **Obstructed Views** Another consequence of our living in a three-dimensional world is that objects can sometimes partially block our view of other objects. When that happens, the boundary of the blocked object can change drastically. In the simplest case of only one object blocking part of another, a computer-vision system would see a boundary that would consist of a piece of the blocking object and a piece of the blocked object. More often, the pattern is more complex than that. In the future, sophisticated computer-vision systems will be needed on planetary rovers, robot vehicles designed to explore other planets where people can't go. In order for these vehicles to move at much faster than a very tired snail's pace, they will need to see and recognize obstacles and to deal with obstructed views.

• **Shadowing** Another problem for the planetary rovers will be recognizing shadows. Dr. Hans Moravec (now at Carnegie-Mellon University), in his pioneering work on robot mobility at Stanford University, discovered that his robot's vision system was confused by shadows. It identified shadows as actual objects and planned its path to avoid them.

• **Moving Objects** Although the objects on the ground in Moravec's experiments were stationary, they would move in the robot vision system's view as the robot moved. One of Moravec's most difficult tasks was to create software that matched objects in the two robot's-eye views before and after it took a "step."

• **Alternate Forms** We learn to recognize an object as a car not only when it is seen from a different vantage point but also when it has a different shape because it is a different model. Recognizing objects that have alternate forms is a challenging problem for computer-vision systems.

of that zip code near the bottom of the envelope. From there on, the letter can be automatically routed to its destination post office by machines that read the bar code.

Some post offices have machines that are able to read the street address and then route the mail to the correct letter carrier automatically, perhaps even arranged in the proper order for delivery. That kind of sorting also happens to a limited extent with mail carrying the nine-digit "zip + 4" code.

COMPUTER HEARING

The information in sound has a very different form from the information in light. This leads to computer-hearing systems which are vastly different in concept and design from computer-vision systems.

The human brain and the computer analyze visual information as a scene viewed all at once. Whether the scene is still, as in a photograph, or changing, as in a movie, it is rich with meaning to us. Sound, in the form of language or music, can also be rich in meaning. Its richness, however, comes not all at once but rather in changes that take place over time. For a human, the "pixel" for sound is not a small area of space but a short period of time.

The computer-hearing systems we will discuss are made to sense sound in the same way as a person does—the "pixels" being very short periods of time. But it is interesting to imagine a different kind of computer sound-sensing system. Since a computer is not limited to two ears, it could have hundreds of sound sensors spread out over a large area to sense a "scene" of sound—a large-scale still picture that could be just as rich in meaning to the computer as a photograph is to us.

Just as we describe a light pixel by brightness and color, we describe a sound pixel by loudness and pitch. A *sound wave* is a vibration that passes through matter, usually air. It consists of small alternating regions of high and low pressure that travel away from a vibrating object.

Our ears respond to both the difference in pressure between alternating regions, which we sense as loudness, and the rate of vibration, which we sense as pitch. Our ears contain pitch-sensing structures that respond to different vibration rates (or frequencies), from as fast as 20,000 per second to as slow as 20 per second.

The structures in our ears respond to each different pitch by producing an electrical signal that travels to the brain along a fiber of the auditory nerve. The stronger the signal in a given nerve fiber, the more of that pitch we hear in the sound. If the sound is coming from a musical instrument, we can recognize its particular blend of pitches as its characteristic tone. The scientific term for the amount of each frequency in such a blend is *spectrum*.

When a person speaks, when a musician plays an instrument, or when something makes noise, the spectrum of the sound constantly changes. The changing of the spectrum, not the spectrum itself, is what carries the information in sounds.

Looking at a voiceprint may give you a better idea of how a changing spectrum carries information and, at the same time, how we can give a computer useful ears.

COMPUTER EARS

A voiceprint machine produces a visible display of a changing sound spectrum. A thin vertical strip on the voiceprint shows the sound spectrum at any one time. A dark area at the bottom of the strip means that the spectrum contains a strong low-frequency portion. A dark area at the top shows a strong high-frequency portion. The darker the area, the stronger is that portion of the spectrum.

Male voices tend to produce voiceprints that are darker in their lower portions. Female voices produce darker voiceprints in the higher portions.

When the voiceprint machine detects a sound, it displays the changing spectrum as a series of vertical strips with the beginning of the sound at the left and later parts of the sound farther to the right. If the sound is short and sharp, like a snapping of the fingers, the voiceprint shows a narrow vertical region of light and dark grays, representing the snap, surrounded by a nearly white region, representing silence.

If the sound is extended, like a shuffling of shoes on the floor, there is gray all across the print. Each sound of a human language has a characteristic spectrum and print. For example, the spectrum for "mmm" is concentrated in the lower-frequency portion of your voice. When you make a hissing sound, you use the high-frequency portion. Letters like *b* and *p* are explosive, so they show up with a sudden increase in darkness as the print goes from left to right. The sounds of *v* and *f* are softer and show up more gradually in the print.

Say "Mom misses Pop" and think about how it might look on a voiceprint. In what ways would the voiceprint be similar and in what ways would it be different if a man and a woman each spoke that sentence?

A voiceprint machine is thus a way to represent

a sound in a way that a person or computer can analyze. It would be a great computer ear if only you changed its output. Simply replace the printer's varying shades of gray with an electrical signal that varies in the same way, and you're ready to feed an image of the sound into a computer.

RECOGNIZING SOUNDS AND SPEECH

If you didn't carry out the "Mom misses Pop" exercise in the last section, do so now. Next, think back to the discussion of detecting and recognizing objects in computer vision. Does that give you an idea of how a computer can learn to recognize sounds and speech?

The patterns in a voiceprint are in many ways similar to the objects in a television image. So enabling a computer to recognize a sound is in many ways similar to enabling it to recognize an object in a television picture.

In some ways, it is easier to teach a computer to recognize speech than to identify objects in a picture. For instance, you don't have to worry about the objects being rotated. And you can use the microphone to limit unwanted sounds.

In other ways it is harder for a computer to recognize words than visual objects. Some words produce very similar voiceprints. Some people speak with accents or have impediments. People speak in a wide variety of pitches. Some people speak fast; others speak slowly.

Despite the difficulties, great progress has been made and continues to be made in speech recognition. Some factory robots respond to voice commands. Some computers accept voice input, making it possible for people with severe physical handicaps to be productive workers. Without question, the development of computers that recognize speech is one of the most significant contributions of AI research.

9

Expert Systems to Understand and Translate "Natural Language"

An American man once asked a Greek colleague to translate the English expression "It's Greek to me!" into Greek. She did so, but, not speaking a word of her native language, he couldn't understand what she said.

So he asked her to translate it back into English. "It's Chinese to me," she said.

They laughed and wondered whether their Chinese-speaking friends had similar expressions in their native language.

AI AND NATURAL LANGUAGES

Two of the most challenging and interesting areas of AI research deal with words and their meaning: the automatic understanding of speech and translation of documents from one "natural language" to another.

If the term *natural language* is Greek to you, then you don't speak "computer sciencese." Because computer scientists deal with many types of invented languages in their work, from programming languages to machine languages, they need an adjective to describe what most people simply call "language." They use the term *natural* to contrast

91

English or Latin with the artificial languages they deal with in their work.

Earlier, you read about a computer ear that can distinguish words or phrases from one another and about reading machines that translate printed words into sounds. But neither the speech recognition machine nor the reading machine deals with the *meaning* of the words to which it responds.

UNDERSTANDING VERSUS RECOGNITION

It's a lot easier to recognize a written or spoken word than to understand it. The following story illustrates that point.

Imagine that your sibling, "The Pest," is playing catch with your family's very fancy robot, "Andrea Android." The robot has AI vision and hearing. "She" is programmed to respond to the sight of a moving object by following it with her "hand" unless she hears a voice command to do something else. Since her "brain" is a computer, she follows the instructions in her program perfectly.

The Pest hears and sees better than Andrea but cannot be depended on to obey your commands. As The Pest throws, you notice that the "ball" is actually your parents' favorite table decoration, a china apple. Andrea responds to the flying object by moving her hand leftward.

"Stop that. Right now!" you yell.

Andrea's hand stops, then begins moving toward the right. The apple smashes to bits against the wall. Just then, your parents come into the room.

"It's all your fault!" shouts The Pest. "Andrea would have caught the apple if you hadn't told her to stop and then to move her hand to the right."

If that story were true, The Pest would be correct. Most speech-recognition systems respond to only a few words, but they don't really "understand" them.

The Pest would understand that "Stop that" means "Stop throwing the apple." Andrea, on the other hand, would simply be programmed to stop moving whenever her speech-recognition system detects the word *stop*.

The Pest would also understand that you said "right" to emphasize "now." Andrea's program, however, might respond to the word *right* by preparing to move her arm in that direction and to *now* by carrying out what she had just prepared to do.

UNDERSTANDING AND EXPERTISE

The main message of that story is that the meaning of a word often depends on its context—that is, on the other words surrounding it. The robot in the story can only stop one thing, its arm, and can only understand "right" as a direction in space, not as a word used for emphasis and not as the opposite of "wrong."

Even if a word or phrase has a single meaning, understanding its connection with other words or phrases may require human experience. For example, if you hear a man say, "I saw the sailor hitting the dog on the head with a telescope," you would probably interpret it to mean that the man was looking through the telescope and that the sailor hit the dog's head. You would do so because you recognize the connection between "saw" and "telescope."

You would develop that interpretation by calling on your expertise at understanding the English language. A computer would need to be programmed with an expert system or decision-support system to reach a similar interpretation.

If the program were developed by a programmer from the navy, it might have a different interpretation of the statement. In common naval slang, the "head" is the part of the ship where the toilets are located. Since the man is talking about seeing a sailor, it is logical to interpret that the event described takes place on board a ship.

If it is a large ship, it could easily have several toilet areas, one of which might have a telescope on its roof. Then the only problem in interpreting the sentence is this: who was located "on the head with a telescope" when the event took place—the dog, the sailor, or the man?

TRANSLATION

Automatic translation of speech and text basically requires the same expert skills as automatic understanding, but with two significant differences. First, an automatic translator must be proficient in two languages. Second, it must be able to turn meaning into words as well as words into meaning. That is a very different skill. As anyone who has studied a foreign language can tell you, learning to read and understand that language is far easier than learning to write or speak it.

Automatic translation of speech is more demanding than translation of written documents. To understand what is said, the speech-recognition system must be able to identify words spoken in a variety of tones in a variety of accents or dialects. Written documents are much more standardized; spoken words are often colloquial and even ungrammatical.

Once the words are recognized, the translation of a written document can proceed at any speed, fast or slow. On the other hand, a speech-translation program must work fast enough to produce speech at a speed acceptable to the listener. That is beyond the capabilities of current computer speeds and translation programs.

10

New Computer Technologies and the Future of AI

This chapter looks into the future of the science and application of artificial intelligence with some help from Professors Simon and Newell, whom you have met earlier.

COMPUTER EVOLUTION AND REVOLUTION

Every year, new computer products come onto the market and into research labs. Most of the new machines are evolutionary; that is, changed slightly, but not fundamentally, from the older ones. Their larger memories and faster computation speeds make them valuable for many applications, including AI.

These evolutionary improvements enable people to consider larger problems and more complex computations. In expert and decision-support systems, for example, expertise can be represented in more detail, and thus programs can produce more realistic guidance to users. Sometimes, increased speed alone is the important factor. Faster computation may make it possible to provide timely AI analysis or advice in rapidly changing situations (such as a hospital patient's condition or an aircraft's location) for which previous computation speed was inadequate.

Some new computer products are not evolutionary but revolutionary. Their hardware or software is fundamentally different from that of any machines that preceded them. The new capabilities of these machines are achieved not by faster circuits and improved memories alone, but by innovative *computer architectures* or software techniques.

FROM SUPERCOMPUTERS TO NEURAL NETWORKS

The term *computer architecture* refers to the way in which the components of a computer system are interconnected. A new interconnection scheme can often result in new or more effective ways of carrying out a computation or performing an analysis. Let's look at a few different computer architectures to understand how revolutionary changes can affect AI.

The information-processing architecture of a standard "general-purpose" computer is simple. There are two main parts connected together: its *memory*, where information is stored, and its *central processing unit*, or *CPU*, where the calculations are carried out. The information-processing power of such a machine is determined primarily by three factors: the size of the memory, the processing speed of the CPU, and the rate at which information can be exchanged between them.

Now suppose an AI program includes a calculation in which 10,000 values have to be averaged together. To compute the average, the CPU computes the sum of all values then divides by 10,000. The total computation time for this is the time for 10,000 additions plus the time for one division.

Computing with Multiple Processors If the computer had a different architecture, with 100 individual processors instead of one central processor, the same problem could be solved much more quickly. The program for such a computer could assign each processor the task of adding 100 of the 10,000 values to produce 100 intermediate sums. Then one of the processors could be assigned the task of adding those intermediate sums and dividing the result by 10,000. Since the processors could work in parallel, in the time that a standard single-CPU computer would calculate only 200 sums, the multiprocessor architecture could calculate all 10,000.

(Actually, the 10,000 sums can be calculated by the multiprocessor computer in the time needed for a standard computer to perform 107 sums. After producing the 100 intermediate sums, the multiprocessor computer can assign fifty processors the task of adding them in pairs. The fifty sums produced in that step can be added in pairs by twenty-five processors. In each step, a decreasing number of processors adds intermediate sums in pairs until a single sum is computed.)

A modern supercomputer has that kind of an architecture: multiple processors sharing a common memory. In supercomputers, each of the several processors is at least as powerful as the CPU of a top-of-the-line standard computer.

Some AI researchers believe that the future of their field depends on massive parallel processing. They work on machines like the Connection Machine, which has 65,536 very simple parallel processors that can be automatically interconnected in a vast number of ways.

A famous parallel machine is the chess-playing HiTech, which once had the lead in the race for the

Fredkin Prize. It has 64 special-purpose intergrated circuit "chips," one for each square of the chessboard. Each chip evaluates moves that would bring a piece to its particular square and then sends its evaluation to a central computer.

Deep Thought, although it has a different architecture from HiTech's, also relies on parallel processing to achieve its million-board-position-per-second rate.

Simon and Newell take a different view of multiprocessor architectures. To them, computer power, however it is achieved, is the key to better AI in all forms.

"We use memory, we use speed, and we use bandwidth, period," Simon says emphatically. (*Bandwidth* is the rate at which information can be transferred from one part of a computer system to another, such as from memory to a processor.) "Almost the only relevance of parallelism is that it allows you to do some things in real time [that is, at a speed that keeps up with other ongoing events] which you might not have been able to do at all. For example, chess is a timed game."

Newell adds that even in real-time situations, a standard computer can be used if it has enough memory, computes rapidly enough, and moves lots of information quickly. Parallelism is just a convenient way to achieve those capabilities.

Neural Networks Another interesting new computer architecture is designed to imitate the human brain. Just as the brain is made up of billions of interconnected neurons, each of which behaves in a relatively simple way, *neural networks* or *neural nets* are systems of simple processors. Each processor is capable of receiving signals from several others. It responds to those signals by putting out a signal of its own. The strength of the connection between any two neural net processors can change with time, just as connections between neurons in the human brain can change.

Many researchers believe that neural networks will be particularly useful for pattern recognition, as in computer vision and hearing. Others believe that they are the key to making machines that learn.

Simon and Newell disagree. They believe advances in pattern recognition and machine learning require not special architectures but simply increased memory and speed of processing and transferring information. Even so, they find neural networks interesting as possible research models because their interconnections can mimic the structure of human brains.

Newell puts it this way: "Neural nets in computer science have two roles. [For psychologists,] there is the 'I'm interested in human cognition [thinking]' role. But [for applications] there is the issue of using neural nets, for instance, in speech processing. There, neural nets are absolutely no different from any other computing device. . . . They are just one other version of this process of how I get this computation power."

Simon goes a step further. "If you look at what are called neural nets in this business, with the exception of very few people who are doing things way down at the neurological level [that is, trying to model a very small portion of the brain], these things don't look at all like brains. They're just very simple parallel computing devices which may be useful for certain kinds of tasks."

FUZZY-WARE

In AI, the most revolutionary computer software may be so soft that it is fuzzy.

A major difficulty with many AI programs is that they are "brittle." They can be quite powerful as long as they are applied in previously explored areas, but when they are called on for a situation just beyond the limit of their previous applications, they fail suddenly and spectacularly, just as a strong but brittle ceramic object can shatter when stressed beyond its limit.

Knowledgeable people who use brittle expert systems smile and ignore the computer when it makes a ludicrous recommendation. But when such a system is to be used automatically, for example, in a pilotless military airplane, its brittleness can cause irrevocable failure.

"Fuzzy logic" is an attempt to replace brittleness with "soft failure." Machines with fuzzy software may deviate from ideal behavior, but the deviation is small enough that it can be corrected. They achieve that behavior by using software that treats numbers not as being exact quantities but rather as having some margin for error.

Since most numbers used in expert and decision-support systems are based on measurements, they are indeed somewhat uncertain. If the measurements are in error, the recommendations of the program will be in error also. Fortunately, their fuzzy logic prevents a small deviation from causing a large change in a machine's response.

Advocates of fuzzy logic say that it is particularly well suited to pattern recognition programs, since an image is almost never an exact match to a known object. When the task is to recognize that object in a scene, the most important question is, How close is close enough? That, they say, is when fuzzy logic may be most useful.

Critics of fuzzy logic say that it is often misused as a substitute for making improvements. They point out that it is still important to do the following: (1) modify heuristic formulas to make them less brittle; (2) use inference engines that can handle rules of the form, If x is true, then it is highly likely that y is true; and, especially, (3) seek all the knowledge available before making a decision.

Simon and Newell view fuzzy logic as somewhat interesting but not really a fundamental breakthrough. They agree more with its critics than with its advocates.

Newell says that fuzzy logic programs are interesting to study for certain types of effects. He also states

[They] clearly have some uses in exactly the way neural nets have some uses. . . . They produce effective computing, just the way neural nets are being used in some speech applications. [But] that's to be distinguished entirely from the conceptual claim that fuzzy logic is a fundamental approach to the nature of uncertainty and ambiguity. [It has no connection to] the real nature of what is happening in humans when they are vague and fuzzy about things.

Simon calls fuzzy logic "a particular way of dealing with uncertainty that probably bears little resemblance to" what goes on in the human mind. As to the claim that fuzzy logic makes AI programs less brittle, Simon agrees that they work, but adds,

"Don't make premature decisions before you've got all the knowledge you can get. . . . Fuzzy evaluation functions don't overcome ignorance; they just suspend belief!"

THE FUTURE ACCORDING TO SIMON AND NEWELL

AI is a field that has grown and changed enormously since its founding, so it's natural to wonder what's next. Almost anything, answer Simon and Newell, and almost everyone—including you—will have something to say about it.

"Ask yourself what things would be needed if people or computers could do them," says Simon.

> You can start working to build systems that do that. That's really the way the field has developed. Some of us think that there is no area which is immune from eventual exploration. The main direction will come from people asking, "Gee, what are we doing now that's a big bother and that we ought to get the help of a computer to do?"
>
> So I would expect—one of the predictions I'm most confident about—that as it becomes clearer that artificial intelligence is applicable to a wide range of human affairs: (a) it's going to be done on multiple fronts at once; (b) most of it's not going to be done by computer scientists or artificial intelligence people; and I can already cite you many, many examples of that. It's mostly going to be done by people in the end-use fields who see a need and who have more-or-less direct contact with these more theoretical sources of ideas.

Newell predicts that AI will soon be as commonly used as computers are today. "Computing doesn't belong to computer science types. It is a commodity which everyone can use; and, because it's expanding what can be done with it, it also expands what people can look at. They can see new ways to do new things."

Simon compares the computing revolution with the Industrial Revolution, which

> *was not dominated by steam engine manufacturers. In the long run, all they were producing was energy. The turning point in computing—there's no single turning point—the point where the center of gravity shifted toward the user end was when the microcomputer and the personal computer came along, and lots of people got hands-on experience.*

Newell continues, picking up the story from his colleague with barely a pause for breath,

> *Before that time, computing was a function only of elite organizations, and they controlled it in the usual organizational way. The mass market for computers was the thing that broke that open. That's actually a historically very critical change in the nature of the field. "Power to the people!" if you want to say it that way.*

The same change is beginning to occur for AI. Simon views the world of knowledge as a pyramid. To build it higher, he says, you have to broaden the base.

> *Most of the public has heard the phrase "artificial intelligence" and they still don't know*

what the hell it means. I encounter that all the time when I give public talks. But there's this larger intermediate group who are beginning to know what it means and make use of it. That pyramid has been growing, and the minicomputer revolution broadened its base— a lot.

You can go all the way back to the sixties when I first arrived on this campus. What did [Computation Center Director and Professor] Alan Perlis do, in his wisdom? What he did, in his wisdom, was to leave the door unlocked to the d--n computer, and students swarmed all over it!

They weren't taught about computing. We didn't have courses in computing. They let the computer teach them! And that's why the minicomputer is so important, because the computer is, in fact, the best communicator of knowledge about computers.

Newell continues

Look at the area of expert systems. This is an area that grew within artificial intelligence. It is now an area which is largely not artificial intelligence. That is, most of the work on expert systems is not being done by people who are trained in artificial intelligence. It's being done by all kinds of technical people. . . .

"Stockbrokers, for example," interjects Simon.

" . . . just like programmers out there in various industries" are not computer scientists, Newell goes on. Expert systems "is now extremely commercial and pragmatic. . . . There's all sorts of expertise being captured." The people who are doing it, he points out, have a fair amount of technical expertise in how to program and deal with expert systems. But "they just no longer are people who come from computer science."

That's right, says Simon. "If you look around this campus, a very tiny proportion of the sophisticated computing is being done by the Computer Science Department." Some of it is being done in surprising places, like the English Department and the Architecture Department. That's why Simon and Newell see the AI pyramid growing tall and—more importantly—broad.

SURPRISES

Since Simon and Newell sensed, from the beginning of their AI work together, that they were onto something big, it is natural to ask whether they have had any surprises. They spoke of two, one positive and one negative.

Referring to the fact that AI businesses took nearly thirty years to develop, Simon said, "The big thing that surprised me, and I think surprised Allen too, was how long it took the gold rush to develop and how few adventuresome spirits we had in academia."

Newell agreed, but had an explanation: "There were a lot of other interesting things going on in computer science."

"On the positive side, one of my surprises was how relatively rapidly progress was made with natural language," Simon continued, with Newell nodding agreement. "At the beginning, I thought that I was one of the really hard ones. . . . I think our main bottlenecks there today are not in natural language, but in our ability to mount projects big enough to grow the data bases that would be necessary to do a job on the full language with all of its possibilities for metaphor."

SOME ADVICE

Simon and Newell concluded the interview with some advice to young people who are considering a career in artificial intelligence. The first step, both agreed, is to get hands-on experience with computing. But more important is to become a complete and educated adult.

Newell put it this way: "After you become fascinated with computers, remember that you also have to get broadly educated in other sciences and other things." He then added an important cautionary note: "It's possible to get totally consumed by computers."

Simon agreed, and closed with his typical enthusiasm: "You don't have to be in computer science to be deeply involved with exciting applications of computers. As a matter of fact, you're going to have a hard time finding a field in which you're not."

Glossary

ANALYTICAL ENGINE: A machine designed by Charles Babbage as the successor to the difference engine. It had all the essential elements of modern computers, including the concept of software. Like its predecessor, it was never built.

ARCHITECTURE: In computer terminology, the word *architecture* is used to describe the general way in which a system is assembled. For example, today's supercomputer architectures have multiple processors, high-speed information-transfer interconnections, and one or more large memory units.

ARTIFICIAL INTELLIGENCE: Behavior by a machine, usually a computer, that would be considered intelligent if performed by a human. Or the science that studies such behavior and machines that exhibit it.

BIT: A digit in the binary, or base 2, system of representing numbers. Its name is derived from *B*inary dig*IT*. A bit can be represented numerically as either zero or one. The binary system is the usual way for electronic computers to deal with information, because they naturally deal with a sequence of on-off signals, which can be interpreted as sequences of those two numerals.

BRITTLENESS: In computer science, the property of a program of failing suddenly and spectacularly when it is used just outside its domain of usefulness. One way of overcoming brittleness is to use fuzzy logic.

BRUTE FORCE: An artificial-intelligence program uses brute force when it relies primarily on the computer's ability to consider a huge number of possibilities. People consider fewer possibilities but generally are skilled at selecting the most promising choices to consider. Today's best chess-playing computers generally use brute force, applying much of their computational power to consider moves that a human expert would automatically reject. The machines are strong players only because they are powerful enough to search deeper than most human players even with this wasted effort.

BYTE: A grouping of eight bits, which is particularly convenient for many computer systems to deal with.

CAPTURING: As used in the language of expert systems, the process of creating a representation of expertise in the form of a knowledge base that the computer can use.

CENTRAL PROCESSING UNIT (CPU): The portion of a computer which carries out the main portion of the information-processing task.

COMPONENT: One of a set of interconnected pieces that work together to perform a task. The combination is called a *system*.

COMPUTER: A machine made up of an interconnected set of electrical, electronic, and mechanical parts, designed to manipulate information and exchange information with other machines or with living beings.

DATA BASE: A large collection of related information. The term usually refers to information in computer-readable form, but that need not be so. A telephone book is a human-readable data base.

DEBUGGING: The process of removing errors from a computer program or system.

DECISION RULES: The part of an expert system that represents the way an expert uses knowledge to make choices. The current situation is compared to the knowledge base in order to determine which rules should be used in making a decision. Then the inference engine makes a judgment or recommendation based on the applicable rules.

DIFFERENCE ENGINE: A machine designed in 1821 by Charles Babbage but never completed. It was intended to improve vastly the computation of mathematical tables used for navigation, among other things.

EVALUATION FUNCTION: A formula used to estimate the strength of a given position in a computer program for playing a game such as chess. The evaluation function enables the program to compare all possible future positions and thereby select the most promising move.

EXPERT: A person who has vast knowledge of a particular area and/or a particular skill.

EXPERTISE: The knowledge or skill that an expert possesses. The realm of that knowledge or skill is called an *area of expertise*.

EXPERT SYSTEM: A computer system designed to make effective use of a knowledge base so that it can provide expert guidance to a user or to another computer system.

FREDKIN PRIZE: A $100,000 reward to be given to the developers of the first computer system that defeats the world chess champion in an official match at least twelve games in length. Two intermediate prizes have already been awarded to the first systems to play at the master and grand master levels.

FUZZY LOGIC: A programming technique that takes the inexactness of measured values into account. It is used in some artificial-intelligence applications to permit recovery when the computer recommends an action and deviates from ideal behavior.

HARDWARE: The electrical, electronic, and mechanical parts of a computer system.

HEURISTIC: Referring to knowledge based on familiar, often repeated, experiences. "Rules of thumb" are based on heuristic knowledge. Some knowledge bases are largely heuristic.

INFERENCE ENGINE: The part of an expert system that makes judgments and recommendations based on which decision rules apply to the situation at hand.

INFORMATION: A pattern that represents a concept or fact. For example, this definition is a pattern of ink on paper that represents an idea in a form that you can read.

KNOWLEDGE: A collection of information about a particular topic.

KNOWLEDGE BASE: Knowledge organized in such a way that the relationships among its facts can be determined by a computer.

KNOWLEDGE ENGINEERING: A field that deals with the methods of creating, manipulating, and using knowledge bases.

MEMORY: In computer terminology, a component designed to store information for later use.

MIND TOOLS: A term used in this book to describe computer systems that use artificial intelligence to enable a person to go beyond the usual limits of human mental abilities.

MOVE GENERATOR: The portion of a game-playing program that produces future board positions that may result from any combination of legal moves and countermoves.

NAPIER'S BONES: A machine invented by John Napier in 1617 that was probably the first mechanical calculator. Unlike the abacus, which merely kept track of the results while the human user's manipulations carried out the arithmetic, Napier's machine itself performed the addition, subtraction, multiplication, and division.

NATURAL LANGUAGE: A computer science term for a language used in ordinary written or spoken communication as opposed to one invented for use with computers.

NEURAL NETWORK or NEURAL NET: A computer architecture composed of many interconnected simple processors that behave similarly to neurons. Its design therefore mimics the structure, and perhaps the behavior, of the human brain.

NEURON: The basic nerve cell of the human brain. A neuron accepts electrical signals or pulses from many other neurons to which it is connected and responds by sending out electrical pulses of its own.

OPTICAL CHARACTER RECOGNITION: A computer technique for analyzing an optical image that leads to identification of letters and other printed characters in it.

PARALLEL PROCESSING: Carrying out different parts of a program in different parts of the hardware at the same time. One way that computer designers gain processing speed is to design their systems to do parallel processing.

PIPSY: A term used in this book to describe a computer. It stands for programmable information-processing system.

PIXEL: A small region of an image produced by a television camera. *Pixel* is a shortened form of *picture element*.

PROCESS: An activity that combines several elements or objects, or changes an element or object, to produce something more useful than what was originally present. Also, to carry out such an activity. A computer processes information.

PROCESSOR: A component of a computer in which information processing takes place. Most of today's computers have only a single processor, which is then called the central processing unit, or CPU. But many new computer architectures, including supercomputers, have multiple processors.

PROGRAM: A set of instructions for a computer that describe how to carry out a particular information-processing task.

SEARCH DEPTH: The number of moves and countermoves into the future that a game-playing computer can consider.

SENSOR: A device used to detect or measure a property of the environment (such as light intensity in a particular direction) and produce a signal that represents that property to the computer. A television camera is usually used as a sensor for computer vision.

SEQUENTIAL or SERIAL PROCESSING: Carrying out a computer program one step at a time, as opposed to using parallel processing. Most standard computers do their work in this way.

SINGULAR EXTENSION: A technique used in game-playing computer programs in which moves that appear to be exceptionally promising are analyzed to a much greater search depth than others.

SOFTWARE: A program or set of programs. The term *software* is used because these programs are as essential to the operation of a computer system as its hardware, yet are quite easily changed.

SPECTRUM: A particular combination of frequencies. In sound, the spectrum of pitches produces the tone we hear. In light, the spectrum of colors produces the shade we see.

SUPERCOMPUTER: A computer capable of carrying out an enormous number of data manipulations in a short time. As the capability of computers is rapidly changing, today's supercomputers will be considered very slow in only a few years.

SYSTEM: An interconnected set of components designed to carry out a particular task.

TURING TEST: The most generally accepted method of deciding whether a computer system is capable of thinking. First suggested by the great British mathematician and computer scientist Alan Turing, it consists of asking questions of an entity, which may be a human or a computer, through a computer terminal and receiving answers from that entity through the same computer terminal. If the entity is a computer, but a human is unable to distinguish its answers from those that another human might give, the computer should be judged to be a thinking machine.

VOICEPRINT: A visible representation of the way the spectrum of a sound changes as time passes.

WETWARE: A term used in this book to describe living brains when they are compared with computer hardware/software systems.

For Further Reading

To me, the best part of writing a book about science and technology is sharing a subject that fascinates me with my readers. Then, after the book is published, my greatest treat is meeting a reader who shares my fascination and wants to know more. Since I probably won't meet you, the next best thing I can do is to tell you about the books I read and enjoyed along my way to writing this one. These books were all written for adults, but you can handle at least parts of them, and you can look forward to growing into the rest. I hope you are up to the challenge of giving them a try.

—Fred Bortz

The Age of Intelligent Machines, by Raymond Kurzweil (MIT Press, Cambridge, Mass., 1990), is an outstanding overview of artificial intelligence and robotics. It is rich with photos, illustrations, and fascinating essays by leaders in AI research and AI business. Although Kurzweil is an expert, he writes clearly in language suited for nonscientific readers. He presents the exciting history, present, and future of his field. But best of all, he presents the interesting people who have shaped it and will continue to do so.

Machines Who Think, by Pamela McCorduck (W.H. Freeman, San Francisco, 1979), is one of the first popular books about artificial intelligence. Despite this book's age and the rapid growth of the AI field, it is still valuable today. It can give you great insight into the minds and thoughts of the founders of AI, and even into the minds and thoughts of the field's greatest critics. McCorduck will take you along with her on her own discovery of the field and will give you a chance to form your own answers to her most interesting questions.

The AI Business: Commercial Uses of Artificial Intelligence, edited by Patrick H. Winston and Karen A. Prendergast (MIT Press, Cambridge, Mass., 1984), is a collection of chapters written by some of the first people to find practical applications of AI. It's an interesting look at the earliest mind tools through the eyes of their creators.

The Rise of the Expert Company: How Visionary Companies Are Using Artificial Intelligence to Achieve Higher Productivity and Profits, by Edward Feigenbaum, Pamela McCorduck, and H. Penny Nii (Times Books, New York, 1988), like the preceding book, focuses on practical applications of AI, especially expert systems. In the four years between the publication of the two books, AI grew from an interesting field with some commercial possibilities to a thriving small industry.

Mind Children: The Future of Robot and Human Intelligence, by Hans Moravec (Harvard University Press, Cambridge, Mass., 1988), is fascinating, entertaining, and deliberately provocative—perhaps even outrageous. Moravec masterfully persuades his readers to peer through the window of his fertile imagination at a sometimes frightening but always intriguing future—where the best minds in the world are our creation, but not ours.

The Emperor's New Mind, by Roger Penrose (Oxford University Press, Oxford, England, 1989), takes the point of view that computers don't think and never will. I found it far harder to read than Moravec's book, and certainly less imaginative. But imagination sometimes can take us beyond the possible, and it is always valuable to consider an opposing point of view. So this book is worth knowing about.

In *The Society of Mind* by Marvin Minsky (Simon & Schuster, New York, 1986), one of the originators of the science of artificial intelligence thinks about thinking. The book is as much about minds as machines, and it begins boldly with these sentences: "This book tries to explain how minds work. How can intelligence emerge from nonintelligence? To answer that, we'll show that you can build a mind from many little parts, each mindless by itself." Its organization matches its theme. Each short section begins on a separate page, and each is a small nugget of an idea or concept. As you read, you build connections between them until Minsky's grand ideas emerge from many little pieces of thought.

Models of My Life, by Herbert Simon (Basic Books, New York, 1991), is the autobiography of a political scientist who is a professor of psychology, and won the Nobel Prize in economics, yet who will probably be best remembered as one of the creators of the field of artificial intelligence. Although much of Professor Simon's life story cannot be appreciated until after the reader has attended college, parts of it can be enjoyed by everyone. I especially liked Simon's stories of the very human aspects of life as a scientist and his insights into the way scientific knowledge develops and grows.

Alan Turing, the Enigma, by Andrew Hodges (Simon & Schuster, New York, 1983), is a long, scholarly, but still interesting biography of the great British mathematician. Like Simon's book, much of this one cannot be appreciated without having experienced college. It describes, among other things, Turing's crucial contributions to the Allies in World War II, when he led the team that developed Colossus, a machine that decoded secret German messages, in a project called "Enigma" (meaning mystery or puzzle). Turing himself was viewed as somewhat of an enigma. After his homosexuality was made public, he suffered extreme punishment and humiliation. He committed suicide in 1954.

There are also a number of biographies of Charles Babbage and books about his difference engine and his analytical engine. I am fascinated by his compulsions and creativity. The man you see browsing in the "B" section of the biography shelf in your library someday may be me, selecting a book about Babbage.

INDEX